Adoption and Spirituality
A Practical Guide and Reflections

By
John D. Rudnick Jr.

About the Author

John D. (Jack) Rudnick, Jr., and his wife, Kathleen (Cranley) are the parents of three children. A native of Boston, Massachusetts, and a U.S. Navy Medical Service Corps veteran, he received a Bachelor of Science degree from Providence College, Providence, Rhode Island, and a Master of Arts in Health Care Administration from The George Washington University, Washington, D.C. He has published numerous articles for professional health-care journals during his 25 year career in health services management which have included responsibility for several children's social services related programs. Jack traveled to China to complete the adoption of their youngest daughter and is a frequent speaker on the topic of international adoption. He recently joined his family's business, The Willis Music Company, Florence, Kentucky, as its business development director.

The Rudnick family—Kathy, Jack, Katie, Jonathan, and Jane live in the northern Kentucky town of Wilder. Jane, their adopted daughter from China, joyfully joined them in 1996 and became a United States citizen in 1999.

Adoption and Spirituality: A Practical Guide and Reflections
Library of Congress Catalog Card Number: 0-108785

ISBN 0-87718-999-4

Publisher Data by Subject Areas:
1. Adoption-international/domestic. 2. Infertility
3. Spirituality/Religion

Limited Edition

Printed in the United States of America

CONTENTS

DEDICATION

With love to Kathy, Katie, Jonathan, Jane, and, Jane's courageous "Birthmother"

ACKNOWLEDGMENTS

At the outset, I am grateful to God, the Holy Spirit, for descending to give me the wisdom to write this book. Many others have played such an important role to make our adoption and development of this book possible. On behalf of my family, I appreciate the prayers and support provided during our process.

I am especially grateful to: our parents – Ed, Jack, Jane, Theresa – for the love, generosity, and support they provide; Katie and Jonathan for the selfless sharing and heartfelt love for their sister; our siblings and their families – the Cavanaughs, Cranleys, Flottmans, Hoods, Luebbers, and Walshes – for their prayers, encouragement, and genuine interest; our close friends, Debbie and Steve Shaner who helped me care for Jane while I was in China and who have been a tremendous source of support and friendship since; the staff at Mid-South Christian Services and Bethany Christian Services – Debby Marston, Sue Murton, Janet Lawrence, and Shiyan Zeng — who provided tremendous time and resources during our process; Jim Dockins, Judy Hamer, Kathleen McLaughlin, Reverend William J. Parham, and Sr. Mary A. Hession, for review of this book and editorial comments; Celeste Aud, Valerie Daugherty, Sandy McLemore, Jim Moss, Gale Parks, Mary Pillow, Kathy Ross, Currie Sanders, Beverly Ward, and Dennis Williams helped a great deal with book preparation for publishing; Thomas Aud, Linda Farmer, and Becky Parks for their library support, expertise, and guidance; and the Alford, Bargiacchi, Keating, King, Martini, and McManus families for "being there" to help with Jane during her first months at home.

FOREWORD

June 23, 2000

Jack Rudnick, Jr.
708 West Forest Avenue
Jackson, TN 38301

Dear Jack,

I am forwarding my "author comments" for your manuscript. (and) I am very flattered that you thought enough of me to ask for my comments, and they are as follows:

"…Written from first hand experience, Jack has provided an excellent tool to guide anyone through international adoption. His insight will give you a clear understanding of this challenging process. The Bible tells us to "Pour out your heart like water before the face of the Lord; lift up your hands toward Him for the life of your children." (Lamentations 2:19) This is what Jack has done and now he is showing us how too."

Jack, I was very impressed with what I read. Congratulations on your personal triumph into the international adoption scene. God has done a mighty work in you and your family. Jane is a very blessed little girl, as all of you are.

May the Lord bless you and keep you and cause His face to shine upon you.

Kindest Regards,
THE LAMPO GROUP, INC.

Dave Ramsey
President

DR/lad

PREFACE

God has truly blessed my life with a great family, friends and career. I have a loving mother and father and a devoted husband of twelve years. I began my legal career in private practice focusing on family and criminal law. Adoptions were always the most rewarding aspect of my practice, although, I must admit, I was envious of the families who were lucky enough to adopt. In 1998, I was elected General Sessions Judge, Division II, for Madison County in West Tennessee. My jurisdiction includes presiding over all legal matters involving juveniles. Once again, I have enjoyed working with parents and children in need. The plight of abused and neglected children has always touched my heart.

During my judicial campaign, a fortuitous meeting occurred... one that would change my life forever. Kathy and Jack Rudnick, Jr came to a neighborhood gathering with the most beautiful Chinese baby girl I had ever seen. Steve and I had contemplated adoption at different times in our marriage, but it finally became apparent that it was God's will for us to begin the lengthy process of adoption and travel to China to get our precious daughter, Clare Burns. We know God placed the Rudnicks in our lives at the right time and, with their help, we have been blessed with the most precious gift of all, a healthy, happy baby girl.

This book will be an invaluable tool for any family considering adoption. It provides insight and wisdom to a process that requires volumes of paperwork, patience, and prayer. I enjoy my role as attorney and judge, but I take greatest pride in being called "Mama."

Judge Christy R. Little
General Sessions,
Division II
Madison County, TN

Clare Little and parents Christy and Steve.

9

INTRODUCTION

One of the greatest joys in life is sharing good news and entertaining stories with friends. Recently, I read that *Reader's Digest* is so popular because of its readers' tremendous interest in the personal stories shared by contributing authors.

I wrote *this* book because of the curiosity and intrigue shown by many surrounding our youngest daughter's adoption. When we began our application process in August 1995, international adoption was rapidly growing for both married and unmarried individuals who considered this over the likely alternative, domestic adoption. (In a sense, we were "blazing a trail," for those who would follow.)

Within an incredibly short time-frame from the start of our processing through adoption, I flew overseas in January 1996 to pick up Jane — a (randomly assigned) seven-month-old infant, then named Su-Qing (pronounced Su-Ching), — from China. Because my wife and our two children remained at home while I traveled with a group of six others who were also adopting, I maintained a detailed journal of my experiences – facts, feelings, and emotions – to share with them. (This journal would also be a legacy for Jane when she was older.)

I strongly feel that there are profound teachings and correlations between adoption and the Bible. From historical and spiritual perspectives, the need to write about important events is highlighted in the Bible. After the Battle of Amalek, God commanded Moses to "write this down in a document as something to be remembered…" (Exodus 17:14). Our adoption of Jane qualifies as a significant event in our lives worth documenting!

With the growing level of local and community interest in our international adoption process, I originally considered writing an article for an appropriate journal in which I would share a "how to" process with expectations and considerations about our experience. (I did write a human-interest article about our experiences for a local

Memphis, Tennessee newspaper, *Common Sense.)* As further requests for information continued, I considered cataloging these questions and including them in an expanded article. While reviewing my journal to prepare an outline, I realized that there were entries "heavily sprinkled" throughout which created a common, continuous theme – recurrent mention of my reliance on faith and prayer. Out of curiosity, I researched bookstores, the internet, and queried publishers to find possible religious-oriented works on adoption (since I observed that most parents we knew had incorporated faith into their adoption consideration). I determined that there was limited material dealing with the *spiritual dimension* of the process. With prayerful consideration and recognition that there was too much for an article, I decided to expand my focus and address this unmet need (on the spirituality of adoption) through this book. I am humbled that God chose me as his instrument to explore this which also partially fulfills His direction for me! Because some contend that no one can "fully" convey an experience to another but can only reflect on the experiences, it is a story of my reflections that I share with you.

* * *

Sometimes it is patently clear when God comes to help us rearrange our priorities and values to make us aware of someone in need. This is a challenge posed to us for, simultaneously, helping others as well as resulting in a closer relationship with God. For my family, the message became clear after prayerful discernment and consideration with a resignation to God's will. The Bible, the major written vehicle through which God speaks, helped shape our decision making and realize His desire for us which was to pursue adoption as a global apostolic calling: "For I know the thoughts I think for you...to give you a future and a hope. (Jeremiah 29:11); "...search for justice...help the oppressed, be just to the orphan..." (Isaiah 1:17-18).

As you read this and are contemplating adoption or another significant choice in life, and worry or have doubts about making a sound decision, serious soul-searching is a must. As Ralph Waldo Emerson so appropriately wrote – (which helped shape my reflective thinking) — "What lies behind us and what lies ahead of us pales by comparison to what lies within us."

Objective and subjective considerations guiding the structure, process, and outcome – the why, how, and what of international adoption -- are combined with our personal spiritual testimony. This is accomplished in three sections which will each contain a literary inspirational piece and a significant "coincidence" from our journey. (Throughout the book, "I" and "we" are used to reflect the involvement of my wife, Kathy and others.)

In section I, I explore "why" we adopted – who we are, our discernment process, and the unfolding issues we considered and executed. The rationale and chronology of events leading to parenthood are provided. The concepts of "spirituality" and "coincidence" are introduced.

Infertility experienced early in our marriage and failed adoption attempts are sequentially discussed. This section concludes with emotions, expectations, and reflections. We learned that God's direction is made clear in The Bible relative to decision making – "Go sell what you have and give it to the poor and you will have treasure in heaven." (Matthew 19:21)

The "how-to" component of Jane's adoption is detailed in Section II. A description of the requirements we satisfied are outlined in a 25-step flowchart. Noteworthy excerpts from my journal comprise the majority of this section.

Our airport "reunion" from China to the United States sets the sequence for the outcome oriented Section III — "what resulted from this experience." Important events after Jane's arrival, practical advice and select inspirational pieces and scripture capstone the book. (Two different Biblical translations – *New International Version (NIV)* and *The New American Bible* – are used throughout this book.)

Examples of "coincidences" (defined in Section I) are provided at the end of each section. "Reflections" on personal witness and testimony are incorporated throughout to highlight my significant feelings and retrospective thoughts as well as to prompt your thinking.

<u>Moses</u>   exodus 3-4.10

<u>Roots + wings.</u>

<u>Birth parents.</u>

<u>orphanage.</u>

*It takes a lot of courage
To put our lives in God's Hands;* Be still
*To give ourselves completely -
Our dreams, our hopes, our plans;
To follow where He leads us
and make His own our own;
But all it takes is foolishness
To go the way alone.*

No <u>greater</u> love — b. parents

Mama   *Anonymous*

The Shack   adopted
                 heirs
                 (Romans 8:16

Conversion

What size shoes
13

Starfish Poem

As I walked along the seashore
This young boy greeted me.
He was tossing stranded starfish
Back to the deep blue sea.
I said, "Tell me why you bother,
Why you waste your time this way.
There's a million stranded starfish
Does it matter, anyway?"

And he said, "It matters to this one.
It deserves a chance to grow.
It matters to this one.
I can't save them all I know.
But it matters to this one,
I'll return it to the sea.
I matters to this one,
And it matters to me."

Anonymous

I.

Why We Adopted

"For we are taking pains to do what is right not only in the eyes of the Lord but also in the eyes of men." (2 Corinthians 8:21)

Adoption Background

Historical

A major reason people adopt relates to "infertility" – the inability for couples to produce a child biologically. Other possible reasons include:

- A child's parent(s)' death;

- Addicted or dysfunctional parents not able to adequately or appropriately care/provide for a child — emotionally or financially;

- Fulfilling an altruistic need for a child born out of wedlock or left orphaned by other unfortunate circumstances;

- A difficult to place "'special needs" child (disabled, a set of siblings, an older child);

- A woman is too ill or has a condition that could compromise her health or the child's by carrying a child in her womb.

Current Trends

Adoptions by single parents and families already with children are rising. In many instances international adoption is the response for those interested resulting from a heightened awareness of the global need for loving adoptive families. This movement has also been driven, in large part, by removal of global political, economic, and sociological barriers with an increased belief in a universal sense of "connectedness." (Mother Teresa adamantly disagreed that there is an overpopulation problem in the world. She once shared that "It is foolish to think there are too many children...that is like saying there are too many flowers!") The consistent rise in international adoption in the United States, also lies in the desire, by families, to become more fulfilled emotionally, and spiritually as well as an awakening that there is more to life than unbalanced work, leisure activities, or material goods.

Decision-Making

The adoption decision-making process is achieved in different ways. It is not easy to determine practical likelihoods and the right thing to do. Our family learned that the discernment process to con-sider this "calling" involved several methodologies:

- Assessing objective information;
- Determining who we feel we are by assessing values and self-readiness;
- Being brutally honest about the complex dimensions of our call-ing;
- Invoking spiritual determination through guidance from God.

The combination of these along with the removal of much of the past sociological stigma associated with inter-racial adoption has helped promote this movement. The effort is also furthered by the growing recognition that children are a generous gift from God not to be taken for granted. Decisions to carefully arrange and plan a family around financial stability and "on track" careers can be risky — waiting has resulted in disappointment for many couples. Reasons can include: that infertility with either partner has not been previously detected or recognized; or, simply the fact that chances for conception diminish because fertility decreases with age.

A cycle of frustration then occurs because:
- There is a dwindling supply of infants — especially healthy Caucasian infants;
- There are challenges (e.g. legal concerns) and the expense associated with private placement adoptions;
- There are age ceilings established by domestic agencies which limit the options for those wishing to adopt domestically.

International adoption then becomes a more attractive option because of a plentiful supply of children and most countries' requirements are more liberal. Oftentimes, however, this option is not attainable because those interested cannot afford the steep expenses of the process.

Risks

There is no denying that there are risks associated with adoption (just as there are risks associated with having children who are conceived biologically). Risks with international adoption include:
- Genetic uncertainty of the medical, developmental, or social

history of a child;

    • Uncertainty about the intellectual potential of the child;

    • Concern that the bond of emotional attachment may be difficult to establish – especially the older the child is when adopted.

In addition to an abundance of available children, a strong advantage of international adoption is avoidance of the emotional heartbreak that occurs if a natural parent changes his or her mind within legally established periods of time. Discussion concerning other viable birth options – in-vitro fertilization, artificial insemination, or birth by a surrogate mother – (which are controversial from legal, moral, and religious perspectives) is not considered in this book.

Religion and Spirituality

This spiritual dimension of adoption about which little has been formally written involves personal faith and a spiritual relationship with God. As we reflect on *why* we adopted, most of our reasons were centered around:

    • Our religious faith and personal spirituality;

    • Trust for the future through "divine providence";

    • The happiness already experienced with our two older children as "gracious gifts from God."

Children are a vehicle through which God makes Himself known to us as well. "…whoever receives the one I send, receives me, and whoever receives me receives the one who has sent me." (John 13:20). Children are privileged blessings not to be taken for granted. The joy of parenthood including our adoption has exceeded our expectations.

Reflection — Spirituality

The increase in spirituality, a powerful dynamic of the decision making process, is vital when considering adoption. Faith in God through structured religion (or other ways of recognizing the existence of a higher power) contributes to the means by which people finalize decisions. We learned that adoption is a process – not an event that just occurs "overnight."

18

Our Family–Values And Principles

Why were we drawn to adoption after a 10-year gap between this and our biological children? *What* prompted our "call to action?"

To make a long story short, we were a conventional middle-class family – not one you would probably see featured in *Parade Magazine* or on the Oprah Winfrey Show. We practiced our religion consistently but, admittedly, more actively when children came along. The increased interest in our faith came with age, maturity, and our broadened socialization communities. Kathy and I each had structured religious education classes through our elementary, high school, college years and participated in church-based social activities. Our families each instilled in us the positive virtues necessary for living a good life with an emphasis on the importance of prayer.

Infertility

Early in our marriage we received a "wake up call" about planning – that total control is beyond our capabilities. We had wanted to start a family immediately and were perplexed and frustrated that "nothing had happened" six months after our marriage. We sought medical professionals' advice but they were not overly concerned -- "...relax and don't worry." However, after 18 months we pursued diagnostic testing. At first I was told that I was the problem and was referred to specialists. Little was being done, aggressively, for male infertility in the 1980's let alone discuss it openly. I was placed on an experimental drug to improve chances for conception. It provided some hope in the midst of complex variables associated with a chance to achieve a successful pregnancy. Simultaneously, with Kathy approaching 30, the "ticking of the biological clock" was a significant concern. She underwent two exploratory laparoscopic surgeries six months apart. One fallopian tube was slightly obstructed, but nothing else very remarkable or problematic was determined. Early on during the infertility testing, one obstetrician suggested that we consider artificial insemination by donor. (Because of our religious beliefs, this was not an option we wanted to consider. A lesson we learned from this, however, is the need to be informed and prepared concerning various treatment options before participating in procedures with possible moral, ethical, and emotional effects.)

We placed our name on domestic adoption agency waiting lists since it was at least a three-year wait for a healthy Caucasian infant – our preference at that time. In addition, we prayed, continued to pursue "clinical testing," and tried to manage our intense frustration. This was extremely difficult. We shed many a private tear in our house. "We kept the faith" and persistently chased simultaneous strategies. We worked through it all and regrouped in retrospect, with borderline desperation. While we experienced "failures" each month, family and friends were achieving successful pregnancies seemingly "effortless." My sister, married after us, even had triplets while we waited.

After we relocated to Dayton, Ohio, friends told us of an infertility specialist who seemed to have the "Midas touch," Dr. David McLaughlin. They convinced us to consult him for another opinion. Dr. McLaughlin's initial plan was to conduct compatibility testing on us. Based on this he ruled out incompatibility. He wanted to pursue a hunch through additional diagnostic surgery on Kathy and hopefully find a problem perhaps undiagnosed by other physicians. From this surgery, he diagnosed concrete evidence of the probable (non-life threatening) problem – severe endometriosis – an inflammation of the tissue in the uterus and around the ovaries. The plan was to conduct two subsequent additional surgeries to help correct the inflamation. The first, a major procedure was intended to remove inflamed tissue. The second, three months following, would be diagnostic. With direct application of a medication to the uterine lining, his patients had experienced marked success with conceiving. Given previous unsuccessful use with the more conservative drug, Clomed, we pursued aggressive use of the fertility drug, Pergonal (after the second surgery) which was also prescribed for use.

Reflection

Through prayer, we recalled that The Bible addresses infertility. We related first hand to the gnawing pain and tension experienced by Abraham and Sarah (Genesis 16:1-3). (Their circumstances, we feel, were even more difficult because they did not have clinical treatment or advanced technology which, at least, offered some hope for us!) Also after many years of Elizabeth being barren, an angel through an annunciation communicated to Zechariah that they would soon become parents. (Luke 1:5-8). John the Baptist was born their son.

In his letters to the Thessalonians, Paul advises us to engage in appropriate conduct through constant prayer "...never cease praying..." (1 Thessalonians 5:17). Prayer was the primary coping mechanism we employed in response to the test of infertility. We reflected on the meaning of our faith along with the foundation of the values, principles, and teachings built upon throughout our years of religious formation. It was through our challenges that we learned more about ourselves and each other. We absorbed and applied religious principles to foster the development and further the growth of our spirituality.

Reflections – Humility, Infertility, Encouragement

Infertility quickly humbled us and brought us to our knees. During this difficult period, we sought answers to questions which included:

- *"Why are we being punished?"*
- *"What did we do wrong?"*
- *"When or will pregnancy happen?"*
- *"Can we bargain with God to earn a child?"*

We pleaded for some sign. Our prayerful responses to despondency involved listening for God to speak to our hearts, and pursuit of actions consistent with how we thought and hoped God wanted us to act. We admitted we were helpless without Him and needed Him more than ever in our lives. Reflections on God's messages relative to humility, infertility, and encouragement helped shape our actions:

Humility

- *"Humble yourselves before the Lord, and he will lift you up."* (James 4:10)
- *"God resists the proud, but gives grace to the humble."* (James 4:6)
- *"Humility and the fear of the Lord bring wealth and honor and life."* (Proverbs 22:4)
- *"The humble shall see this and be glad; and you who seek God, your heart shall live."* (Psalm 69:32)

Infertility

- *"Sarah said to Abram, the Lord has kept me from bearing children."* (Genesis 16:2)
- *"...Hannah was childless."* (1 Samuel 1:3)
- *(Jacob to Rachael) "Can I take the place of God, who has denied you the fruit of the womb?"* (Genesis 30:2)
- *"The barren wife bears seven sons."* (1 Samuel 2:5)
- *"But they had no child because Elizabeth was barren and both were advanced in years."* (Luke 1:7)

Encouragement

• *"Ask and it will be given to you; seek and you shall find; knock and it will be opened to you."* *(Matthew 7:7)*

• *"Keep up the good work and don't get discouraged for you will be rewarded."* *(2 Chronicles 15:7)*

Adoption – A parallel process

During our period of infertility testing, Kathy's clinical evaluations for surgery, and the aggressive infertility drug use for Kathy, we pursued domestic, international, and private placement adoption options aimed at expediting our journey to parenthood. With the 3-year wait for a domestic adoption we felt self-imposed pressure to accelerate our efforts. The need to aggressively press on was also in response to an objective reality – that we were precariously approaching the age limit to adopt an infant for virtually all of the domestic agencies we contacted. (International adoption was not a popular option nor as readily available in the early 1980's. The credibility, reliability, quality of service, relatively high expense, and some countries' requirements for establishing a 30-day residency for adoptive parents were disadvantages that made this option unattractive to us at the time.) In late 1982 and mid 1983 our hope turned into optimism with two "private placement" adoption opportunities.

With the first, there was a child born in the newborn intensive care unit (NICU) in the hospital where Kathy worked. The single mother had no insurance and wanted a professional couple with her same religion to adopt the child. A further stipulation included the requirement that the couple pay all hospitalization and healthcare expenses for the mother and the baby. We were excited about being "chosen" by her and pursued the process with full force. This included procuring the services of a local attorney, Steve Pfarrer. I sold my college ring (gold prices were very favorable for selling then) to defray the initial legal expenses. We also decided that if needed we could sell one of our two cars. Kathy, a registered nurse, had returned to school full time to complete her bachelor's degree and was working only part-time — money was tight. In compliance with the state law in Ohio, at that time, we placed the baby (already named Andrew) in a foster home while Steve systematically filed required paperwork. He placed a routine ad in the newspaper in an attempt to notify the father, publicly that he had a child. This was a legal requirement. It was also aimed at protecting us from future recourse the father might have as a result of failure to exhaust all efforts to find him as a natural parent.

The father did respond to the ad. When learning that *he* had a son, the father decided to assume custody. We were very disappointed and saddened; but, we realized that we needed to be accepting and move on.

Six months later we became aware of another scenario where a single mother wanted to offer her child to a loving couple for adoption. "Open adoption" was popular at the time. A young single woman from South Carolina, referred by one of our Navy friends came to live with us. Her intent was to place the child with us for adoption in return for covering her expenses. (Her selfless decision demonstrated courageousness by choosing life instead of the easier alternative — abortion.) Initially, I rejected the "open-adoption" idea for fear that the mother or father would change their minds; but over time, relented and let myself get excited about this prospect. Kathy and I spent time decorating the room and bought furniture and supplies in anticipation of our arrival. After living with us for approximately four months, the mother had a change of heart. One day she informed us, with bittersweet emotion, that she wanted to move back to South Carolina and keep the child. Needless to say, we were devastated. Despite our disillusionment, frustration, and feeling of rejection we processed through our hurt and anger by praying harder. We felt God was testing us similar to his test for Abraham to sacrifice his only beloved Isaac. We hoped that He would miraculously snatch us from our perilous path as He did for them. (Gen. 22:1-19; Heb. 11:17, James 2:20-23)

One month later, with the feeling we had been "brought to the brink," the fertility drug, Pergonal, from injections I administered to Kathy proved successful – we joyously learned that Kathy was pregnant. We were happy, but were not "out of the woods" yet. A further test of our desire for children came with several pregnancy related complications: premature labor at 20 weeks which mandated, for Kathy, three months of bed rest in the hospital on intravenous medication and an additional month at home also on bed rest. She was managed with optimal aggressiveness and the conscientiousness of a specialist in high risk pregnancy, Dr. Jim Huey. Continued tension and stress ensued during the months that followed. Kathy experienced the need for surgery to help manage an "incompetent" cervix; three amniocenteses to determine lung maturity; and, approximately 15 trips to the labor room with false alarms when delivery seemed imminent. After achieving a successful pregnancy to term, we had an unexpected, but fortunately brief, intensive care unit (NICU) stay to treat our first child, Katie's pneumonia. All this reenforced our deep gratitude for this gift of a child. The prayers and patience yielded a successful result.

Three months later, we received the incredibly surprising news that Kathy was, again, pregnant – this time without fertility drugs. A set of challenges somewhat similar to the first followed — bed rest at home (without hospitalization); oral medication; surgery; and, premature labor. Matters this time were complicated with Kathy being on bed rest. We had to send Katie 90 minutes out of town for three months to be cared for by family. Jonathan, our second-born, was slightly premature but healthy. We were reminded to "take nothing for granted!"

Two years later we "tried" for a third child. Kathy even had another diagnostic laparoscopy – her ninth pregnancy related surgery — but no problems were found. We accepted this and counted our blessings with the two children we had.

Reflection – Perseverence
Somehow, we feel rewarded for our total trust and faith in God. "Now if you obey me fully and keep my covenant, you will be my treasured possession." (Exodus 19:5) The stories in Exodus inspire all humanity to face difficulties courageously and continue a strong religious commitment and faith in God. We are grateful for our good fortune:
- *"Consider it pure joy, my brothers, whenever you face trials of many kinds." (James 1:2)*
- *"For nothing is impossible with God." (Luke 1:37)*

"Wounded Healers"

In 1995, we advised close friends, Debbie and Steve Shaner, concerning their challenges and options associated with infertility. Suddenly we felt like "wounded healers" – a term coined by author, Henri Nouwen. He strongly felt that by sharing the pain of a same "wound" with fellow human beings, we can serve and help heal them from our wounds. (Nouwen, 1979) We candidly shared almost five years of infertility experiences, thoughts, feelings, and emotions with the Shaners and, as a result, they embraced adoption as their response to infertility.

Reflection — Wounded Healers

Sometimes we encounter challenges or frustrations in life that prompt us to ask - "Why me, Lord?" Usually we emerge from these difficulties wiser, more sensitive, and stronger.

In general, our "wounds" often benefit others through the credibility and first-hand empathy that we can share. Jesus Christ, as man, experienced the ultimate suffering. His act of self-sacrifice demonstrated that Christ got through His experience through His salvation and the promise of eternal reward. We can get through our challenges every day as well. By serving and witnessing to others we offer hope through our connectedness and unified focus — heaven. Scripture helps us reflect through many of these tough times if we turn to God in prayer:

• "I would speak in such a way that it would help you. I would try to take away your grief." (Job 16:5)

• "So encourage each other to build each other up..."
(I Thessalonians 5:11)

• "Show mercy and compassion to one another."
(Zechariah 7:9)

Awareness — The Media

We first learned about the plight of the Chinese orphans in early 1995 from a national television documentary featuring the overpopulation challenges facing China. Several weeks later, the story was brought closer to home by a local Memphis, Tennessee newspaper. It reported on one couple's success with an adoption from China. (We immediately passed this information along to the Shaners.)

This article highlighted the urgent need for babies in China to be adopted. Strict birth control policies and a one-child-only practice (with exceptions in some provinces) are aimed at controlling their skyrocketing population. There are distinct cultural differences and values between the U.S. and China. In China, boys are the revered gender as they carry on the family name as well as care for parents as they age. Infant girls are often abandoned either in favor of a woman "trying again" for a boy, or if the pregnancy was unwanted. Reasons for not wanting infant girls include a failure to obtain permission from provincial authorities, who regulate birth control/grant permission to have children or girls represent a prohibited second child. The unwanted children also include special needs children (boys and girls) with developmental disabilities. Some infants are simply abandoned or the life of the child is terminated during or shortly after birth. Severe penalties are incurred for families violating the population control policies and guidelines of the province in which they reside. Curtailment of benefits affects: a family's taxes; access to healthcare; education for children; food grain allowance; and, other rights or benefits unique to their community province.

China is a popular source for adoptive parents because of the abundance of healthy infants. Chinese women take excellent care of themselves, nutritionally and lifestyle - wise, during pregnancy. The incidence of AIDS, hepatitis, and sexually transmitted disease is low. There is also virtual certainty that birth-parents will not seek recourse to recapture custody through a post-adoption change of mind.

The Shaners obtained additional information from a local adoption agency mentioned in the newspaper article — Mid-South Christian Services, Memphis, Tennessee – the Memphis branch of its national parent agency, Bethany Christian Services, Grand Rapids, Michigan. Mid-South initiated and managed the entire application process. We received and completed a character reference form for the Shaners as part of their required documentation. While completing their reference, I pondered how much fun it would be for us to have another baby. Realistically, the idea was on the crazy and reckless side. After all, we were in our 40's, our children were just at the point where we rarely needed a baby-sitter, we had a comfortable three bedroom home where each child had their own room, and we did not have the discretionary $18,000 - $20,000 available in liquid assets to cover adoption expenses. We sent the form in for the Shaners and we resolved to dismiss the idea as only a dream. Or so we thought but, as God tells us, again, through one of His Biblical prophets, "For I know the thoughts I have for you." (Jeremiah 29:11)

Decision Making Framework – Spirituality

Shortly after this consideration, Kathy traveled to visit her family in Northern Kentucky. She casually mentioned my "crazy" idea about adoption to her mother, sisters, and a friend. Their response to her, however, was surprisingly positive. The outcome of that discussion would be Kathy's consideration of all issues: there was a global need for adoptive families for the hundreds of thousands of abandoned Chinese infants – if we were experiencing a "calling" to consider adoption, maybe we needed to do ourselves the justice of at least further pursuing it and exhausting the possibility. This prompted her to call me about these second thoughts.

When she returned, Kathy and I sat down and discussed that what it had really come down to was a test of our religious convictions. How seriously were we willing to live out the gospel messages delivered in church each week and would we step up and actualize our response to God's call? Our parents had instilled in us a set of values complemented by years of religious education. We were still active in a faith that challenges us to basically live in, make, and leave the world a better place than how we found it. Kathy had argued that she was getting older and physically she would be challenged, at age 44, to assume responsibility for a new infant. Her sisters, mother, and friends convinced her that age should not be an obstacle in her consideration. She had stayed in good physical shape and was a "young 44"— who could do it! I agreed. (Scott Peck remarks that it is not so much that we can not or are not able to do something; the issue is more are we willing to expend the time and effort to learn how to do something.) (Peck, 1998)

Would God be pleased with our decision to not fully collect information and further explore the child abandonment problem resulting from over population in China? We knew even though it would be a financial stretch, we were capable of arranging the resources amassed during our 17 years of marriage to pursue this. God tells us "We can enjoy riches but we must put the Kingdom of God first." (Timothy 6:17) We concluded that because we felt a strong inclination to do this, we needed to "play out" the scenario. We resolved to become better informed, pray, and watch for signs from God as he promises: "In every way I have shown you that by hard work we must help the weak." (Acts 28:35) If the doors kept opening with each phase of the process, we would know if it were right to pursue — "...the hand of the Lord will be made known." (Isaiah 66:14)

In the midst of all of this, the Shaners, surprisingly, learned that Debbie was pregnant. They decided to place their "adoption process" on hold. Meanwhile, the doors kept opening as we continued our pursuit. The Shaner's good fortune turned out to be short-lived, unfortunately, as a month later she miscarried. After this, the Shaners reactivated their adoption process. We were able to synchronize the submission of our applications for me to travel to China with them. (As will be discussed later in this book, it *did* work out for us to travel together to the same orphanage).

Reflection

The decision to adopt, by its very nature, includes a spiritual dimension. For us, it came from our individual souls where we had grown to have an ongoing personal relationship with God. (Indeed, spirituality is a set of personal religious beliefs molded, nurtured, and refined by faith. Spirituality blends conscience, virtues, and environmental influences to help shape one's deeds. The process of getting in touch with one's self is important in order to further spiritual development and growth.)

For me, the most gut-wrenching allegation reported in the media about Chinese infants involved the drowning of unwanted babies in buckets of water. While far removed from "my world," the blend of factual and spiritual information about this allegation struck a chord of conscience to prompt and compel action.

Spirituality played an important role in our adoption discernment process. We were moved to help with this global apostolic need. The challenge is the ongoing process of what we are supposed to do to build up God's earthly Kingdom. The Bible offers clear direction on decision-making "You have been given freedom; not to do wrong, but freedom to love and serve each other." (Galatians 5:15)

Financial Considerations

The more serious we pursued adoption, the more creative we needed to be about short and long term financing. The practicality was, "no money, no mission!" An immediate hurdle to overcome was the availability of the up-front monies (approximately $6000) for the adoption. In order to assess our financial strategies, we reviewed a "snapshot" of all debt, savings, and financial commitments (e.g., school, church donations). Our only debt was the house. After systematically reviewing our assets, we found that one of our tax-sheltered annuities — 403(b) — contained a "no-penalty" loan provision for which this situation qualified. The amount available and terms of repayment would comfortably fit within our projected household budget over a five-year payback requirement. This opened the door from a financial feasibility perspective to proceed. We considered the objective questions – "Am I Ready to Adopt" – (see side bar), to help ensure that we were realistically turning over as many stones as possible.

Reflection
"A hundred years from now it will not matter the sort of house I lived in, what my bank account was or the kind of car I drove, but the world may be different if I am important in the life of a child."

–Anonymous

"Am I Ready To Adopt?"

• I feel comfortable going public with my adoption plan.

• I'm okay with the idea that my child won't be patterned after me.

• I'm feeling okay about myself—accepting all of me (even the infertility part!).

• <u>Both</u> of us are feeling ready to go forward with an adoption plan.

• (If single) I've considered and found an appropriate opposite sex role model for my child-to-be.

• I've looked honestly at the finances of adopting and parenting, and feel comfortable with them.

• I've thought about what I expect from this child, and what I'm prepared to give. I'm not expecting this adoption to make me pregnant, to fix a bad marriage, or to fill an empty life.

• I've looked at all the elements this child will bring to my family (religious, racial, medical, ethnic), and am ready to accept him/her with them, not in spite of them.

• I admit that adoption is a second choice—I would have chosen to bear my own child. But it's a choice I am embracing.

• I no longer avoid the baby departments of stores, children's birthday parties, and showers. I can fantasize about naming a baby, decorating a room, being a parent without bursting into tears.

• I have time to spend with a child, and want to make time in my life for a child. My lifestyle accommodates children.

• I'm ready to make the time, money and energy sacrifices necessary to be a parent. To make them willingly and lovingly, because this is what I want to do.

• I realize that adoptive and birth parenting are not the same, that there are losses for everyone and gains for everyone, and I'm prepared to accept the extra challenges involved in this role.

• I can imagine my child not just as a baby, but as a toddler, a teen, and adult. I realize that my parenting role will last a lifetime.

(From: "Winning at Adoption," 1990 The Family Network)

Reflection

Based on our experiences to adopt, it is normal to expect doubt, anxiety, and worry about such a significant decision. During this process we received "signs" validating out intentions. An encouraging inspiration was taped to the computer of a clerk's desk at the police station in Bartlett, Tennessee (where we were fingerprinted for the FBI clearance required as part of the process). Mother Teresa was still alive at the time and enjoyed an admiration and notoriety then as she does today. Her practical wisdom demonstrates deeply human spirituality laced with humor – "I know God won't give me anything I can't handle, I just wish He didn't trust me so much!"

Scripture offers further examples and decision-making advice. Examples of trust, belief in God, maturity, and timing are illustrated in The Old Testament. Hope and encouragement are revealed through these teachings illustrated about those who have gone before us. (Romans 15:4-5)

We learned about the tests of frustration and the need for patience - - waiting and asking "why." From my past readings, I recall that a French author, Weil, wrote that waiting patiently in expectation is the foundation of the spiritual life. The spiritual life is a patient waiting. We experienced the very human emotions triggered by wanting things and circumstances. Infertility is one example of our waiting. Patient waiting would prepare for personal maturity in dealing with tough situations later in life. The waiting reminds us that we must continuously pray for what we want and be willing to accept the answers God provides. I strongly contend that had we not experienced the challenges of infertility and failed adoptions, we would not have been sensitized enough to experience our "call" to adopt.

Reflection — Decision Making Guidelines

Life has become so complex and chaotic that decision making and priority setting are oftentimes difficult. Emotional feelings contribute to anxiety and stress. We feel fortunate to have the spiritual guidance offered in the Bible and the role models of virtuous ancestors we admired.

Through meditation, prayer, and reflection on desired outcomes, we attempt to make the best decisions with acquired knowledge and maturity which recognizes environmental considerations (i.e., those issues outside our ability to control). Significant guidance comes from numerous Bible verses on decision making and the "Peace Prayer" of St. Francis of Assisi:

- *"I am your servant; give me discernment that I may understand your statutes." (Psalm 119:125)*
- *"For I want you always to see clearly the difference between right and wrong." (Philippians 1:10)*
- *"My son, pay attention to what I say; listen closely to my word." (Proverbs 4:20)*
- *"To everything there is a season, a time for every purpose under heaven." (Ecclesiastes 3:1)*
- *"Let your good sense guide you." (Philipians 4:4-9)*
- *"Give to your servant an understanding heart to judge your people that I may discern between good and evil." (I Kings 3:9)*
- *"Listen closely to what I am about to say. Hear me out." (Job 13:17)*
- *"Give me an understanding mind so that I can know the difference between what is right and what is wrong." (I Kings 3:9)*
- *"I will give you a wise and discerning heart." (I Kings 3:12)*
- *"Come to me with your ears wide open. Listen for the life of your soul is at stake." (Isaiah 55:3)*
- *"If you cry out for discernment, and lift up your voice for understanding…then you will understand the fear of the Lord and find the knowledge of God." (Prov. 2:3-5)*
- *"Listen well if you would understand my meaning." (Luke 4:35)*
- *"Pay attention and listen to the sayings of the wise; apply your heart to what I teach." (Prov. 22:17)*
- *"Just tell me what to do and I will do it, Lord. As long as I live I'll wholeheartedly obey." (Psalm 119:33-34)*
- *"The Lord God has given us the lands. Go and process it as he told us to. Don't be afraid! Don't even doubt!" (Deuteronomy 1:21)*

Peace Prayer –
Prayer of
St. Francis

Lord, make me an instrument
of your peace.
Where there is hatred, let me sow love;
Where there is injury, pardon;
Where there is doubt, faith;
Where there is despair, hope;
Where there is darkness, light;
And where there is sadness, joy.

O Divine Master, grant that I may not
so much seek to be consoled as to console;
to be understood as to understand;
to be loved as to love.

For it is in giving that we receive;
it is in pardoning that we are pardoned,
and it is in dying
that we are born to eternal life.

Coincidence Defined

It has been said that "coincidence" is God's way of remaining anonymous – part of creation and a tangible reminder to humanity that everything in life bears God's imprint. From a secular perspective, Carl Jung, psychiatrist, coined the term "synchronicity" which he defined as a meaningful coincidence of two or more events when something other than the probability of chance is involved (Halberstam and Leventhal, 1997). Other synonyms I have come across for coincidence include: *luck, chance, fluke, providential, something out of the ordinary, transcendental/spiritual/religious experiences, strange,* and a *random joining of an inexplicable event that defies our sense of the reasonable.*

Coincidence

Once the initial fees were paid committing us to the adoption process, the reality of this important decision "hit home." Our anxiety continued despite our firm belief that we were doing the right thing and fulfilling God's plan. We were excited about the prospect of a third child, yet we had residual doubt and searched for "signs" to validate the correctness of our decision. After all, this was a huge leap of faith. Within a week after committing, we encountered a "personal religious experience – a coincidence." We received, unexpectedly, a check for $3,000 – the exact amount of a required adoption agency deposit. Three weeks later, a second check also unexpected came within $100 of the second $2,600 payment. While seemingly minor, we felt that these were signs of encouragement from God that we were on the right path and needed to trust that He would provide. St. Francis de Sales offers the following regarding anxiety:

Do not fear what may happen tomorrow.
The same loving Father who cares for you today
will care for you tomorrow and everyday.

Either He will shield you from suffering, or He
will give you unfailing strength to bear it.
Be at peace, then, and put aside all anxious
thoughts and imaginings.
... St. Francis de Sales

Legacy of an Adopted Child

*Once there were two women who never knew each
other,*
One you do not remember, the other you call Mother.
Two different lives shaped to make you one.
*One became your guiding star, the other became your
sun.*

*The first one gave you life, and the second taught
you to live it.*
*The first one gave you a need for love, the second
was there to give it.*
*One gave you a nationality, the other gave you a
name.*
One gave you talent, the other gave you aim.

One gave you emotions, the other calmed your fears.
*One saw your first sweet smile, the other dried your
tears.*
*One sought for you a home that she could not pro-
vide.*
*The other prayed for a child and her hope was not
denied.*

And now you ask me through your tears,
The age old question, unanswered through the years,
*Heredity or environment. Which are you a product
of?*
Neither, my darling, Neither.
Just two different kinds of love.

Author Unknown

II.

How We Adopted

Jane Su
July 4, 1995
Changsha, China

"For the Lord watches over the plans and paths of godly men."
(Psalm 1:6)

Support Systems

During our aggressive paperwork completion process, we found that the Mid-South Christian Services staff were supportive, available, and knowledgeable. Our family, friends, work, church community, and the children's school communities encouraged us with questions indicative of genuine interest, encouraging remarks, and the promises of prayer. Our close friends, especially from one local city wide network of friends, "the reunion prayer group," provided ongoing support with their presence and prayer during frustrating parts of the process. (There were also friends who highlighted the many reasons why we should *not* adopt — mainly due to the financial sacrifices we would have to make as well as the infringement on our free time. We did lose close touch with several friends whose values and interests changed from ours.)

Genuine support also came from our families. Initially, we had assumed that because there were already 20 grandchildren between the two families that our adoption would not be as joyous an event as a natural birth. Our families, however, recognized that our hearts were in this decision and they joined in our happiness. (This joy is a tribute to our parents – Ed, Jane, Jack, Theresa – since part of them continues to reside in us and our actions!)

Scott Peck shares that when we are young, our dependency on those who raise us shapes our thinking; and, we benefit in a multitude of ways. (Peck, 1997) Even though we are now adults, and can think for ourselves, we feel fortunate to have had a positive start and a solid base of values on which to build. (Kathy and I do not want to convey the impression that what we did is anything extraordinary. Many others have made unselfish sacrifices under more challenging circumstances. Rather, we feel fortunate to have been chosen to pursue this wonderful opportunity!)

Reflection – Friends
Our Lord helps us build up His earthly Kingdom by giving us communities of friends. Recall that God created man and woman after establishing the world because He was lonely, wanted companionship, and through His generosity wanted to share this tremendous gift of life.

He shared that "it is not good that man should be alone so I shall make him a helper." (Genesis 2:18) It is important that we all have companionship to more fully experience life's blessings; and, that we choose relationships with friends who have a good moral character and will help us focus on a virtuous life. Biblical advice about choices we make in friends is clear. "Be with wise men and become wise. Be with evil men and become evil." (Proverbs 13:20)

A lack of companionship unfortunately, contributes to ongoing social "isolationism" caused by diversions from human interaction through growths in technology, the fear of crime, depression (i.e., the "fear of getting involved,") and other lifestyle choices which foster a lack of "connectedness" and loneliness among people. Failure to join a community results in unresolved social problems, in part, because a "cooperative many" are needed to help resolve complex problems. Loneliness is a problem which is increasing in "epidemic proportions." (Kushner, 1994)

Good friends with values and ideals similar to ours are going to watch out for our overall well-being and help us to engage in appropriate activities. Friends are confidants, sounding boards, and "encouragers." They help show us "the way." The importance of friends is clearly outlined in the Bible:
   • "As iron sharpens iron, so a man sharpens the countenance of his friends." (Prov. 24:17)
   • "A true friend is always loyal, and a brother is born to help in time of need." (Prov. 17:17)
   • "Greater love has no one than this that he lay down his life for his friends." (John 15:13)
   • "The Lord would speak to Moses face to face as a man speaks with his friends." (Exodus 33:11)
   • "You shall love your neighbor as yourself." (Mark 12:30-31)
   • "Be with wise men and become wise. Be with evil men and become evil." (Prov. 13:20)
   • "A man of many companions may come to ruin, but there is a friend who sticks closer than a brother." (Prov. 18:24)
   • "The pleasantness of ones friend springs from his earned counsel." (Prov. 27:9)

Use of Prayer

At one stage of our process, we prayed especially hard during a tense wait for approval of my travel to China. This was part of the process over which I had no control. The approved confirmation of my travel needed to arrive within 24 hours, on one particular day, from China. Otherwise, my trip would have been postponed — likely for another three or four months. The dynamics of the situation — the timing of the letter's arrival, the validation of the visa, and the decision to purchase non-refundable airline tickets ($1,200) created stress and heightened anxiety. (During this period of time – late 1995 and early 1996 — you may recall that the federal government had shut down nonessential support services including the passport division and parts of the INS - - Immigration and Naturalization Services. The paperwork was backlogged and new requests for visas were suspended.) Our plea to God for His intervention was an admission of our helplessness and humanity. We sought this divine intervention in a time of desperation and were fortunate that our prayers were answered. With the persistent follow-through on the part of the staff at Mid-South Christian Services, and Shiyan Zeng, our liaison attorney with the Chinese adoption authority, our goal was achieved. Our prayer request was answered with positive and timely approval. Once again, we felt we were being tested. It reminded us of the need to rely on our Lord and trust his appropriate plan for us.

Reflection – Patience
The following passages helped us cope with our tense situation:
• "For when the way is rough, your patience has a chance to grow. So let it grow...For when your patience is finally in full bloom, then you will be ready for anything, strong in character." (James 1:3-4)

• "...Let us run with patience the particular race that God has set before us." (Hebrews 12:1)

Preparing the Children

Kathy and I carefully identified the significant changes that were about to occur with our family. We took into consideration the needs and perspectives of our anxious children. We decided not to obsess or make an unusually big deal about the unique challenges and differences of adopting. Rather, we chose to be excited as if this were a traditional addition to the family as the children understood from the births of family and friends from school, church, the neighborhood, and extended family members. The main differences explained to them were twofold. Firstly, this would be a short "gestation" period — five months from start to finish. Secondly, a lady would come to our house and conduct a "home study" to determine if our home was a suitable and hospitable enough place in which to care for a special child already born somewhere in China. We explained that "hospitable" means that we should be kind to others less fortunate (than we.) (It is interesting to note that the word "adoption" is from the Latin root "adoptare" which means to choose and to graciously welcome a stranger to become part of the family!) We are reminded of the need for considerate behavior to those with whom we come in contact: "Don't forget to be kind to strangers, for some who have done this have entertained angels without realizing it! Cheerfully share your home with those who need a meal or a place to stay for the night." (Hebrews 13:, 1 Peter 4:9)

Children's Concerns

We feel that our children's concerns were basic and very normal. Examples of honest concerns included:

(Katie)

• Because I am sharing a room with her will she keep me awake?

• Will I have any privacy and will she bother my "stuff?"

• Can I use the family room for sleep-overs with my friends?

(Jonathan)

• I have been the youngest in the family and like it the way it is (i.e., time with Mom and Dad) – Will Jane "take over" all your time?

• Will she bother my toys?

• When I get older, will I have to watch her?

(Both)

• Are we going to be "squashed" in the back seat with a car seat between us?

We involved our children in every step of the adoption decision. It was important to have their buy-in and acceptance as this decision affected us all. Katie and Jonathan actively participated in their new sister's name selection, the adoption arrival announcement, and (Katie only) in arranging the room which was to be shared.

Kathy and I made the conscious decision that she, Kathy, would remain at home to be with the two eager children to stabilize "the household" as well as to save money by her not traveling. I already had a passport and it was assumed that I would be the one (privileged) to complete this journey.

Reflection

The joy, pride, and newfound companionship of an additional sibling far outweighed concerns, adjustments, or sacrifices the children needed to make to welcome and accommodate Jane into our home. (Their reaction to all of this and their response will be further discussed in Section III.)

In retrospect, for Kathy and me, this was an opportunity for us to reflect on our early years with Katie and Jonathan; and to have a "second chance" to raise another child. It would give us the opportunity to do things we may not have been able to do when Katie and Jonathan were smaller — perhaps, due to limited money, time, and experience as parents.

Flowchart

As of this writing, some of the inconveniences and challenges experienced while I was in China in early 1996 have already been addressed and changed. The overall approach we followed at that time, for the most part, remains in place with ongoing efforts to continuously improve the process. A flow chart (see appendix) outlines steps and details the process.

Details

The Dossier

The packet of detailed information and endorsements prepared for the application, including translation of all information into Chinese, is called the "dossier." As broached earlier, we processed our paperwork, working at it hard every day, with compulsive follow up, at a "full-court press" pace. This allowed us to complete our application in just three weeks. Examples of slight hold-ups which may affect others' application process considerations include:

• Requesting early on or having on file original, notarized documents which for us were from other states – our birth and marriage certificates and the children's birth certificates.

• Incomplete documentation of a very minor detail on our application.

• The vacation schedule of a key employee within the Chinese Adoption processing hierarchy.

The Referral

In late November 1995 I received a call at work late one afternoon from the Mid-South office letting me know that a referral

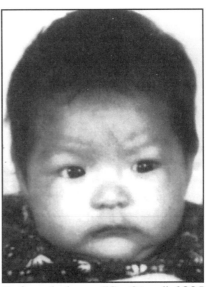

Referral photo, "Su Qing," 1995

photo and supportive paperwork had been received. Debbie Marston, from that office, shared the infant's name, date of birth, and that she was healthy. The excitement began to set in after Kathy picked up the grainy black and white photo and paperwork the next day. For the next seven weeks, we would prepare for my travel overseas and finalize the home needs for our new arrival.

Reflection

(The waiting and preparation for our new infant coincided with the season of Advent which assumed a special significance that season. This sacred and holy time in the church calendar added further meaning and an element of spirituality to our anticipation.)

We each had to give notice at work for time off around my travel itinerary. Both organizations were extremely supportive — we encountered no difficulties with arranging this. While awaiting travel, friends had a baby shower for us, as did our co-workers. This helped tremendously, as we had already donated all of our children's infant and toddler items from earlier years to family and friends.

Reflection

I consulted with the five couples from our area who had traveled to China already regarding what to take as well as "words of wisdom," gained through their experiences. Since I was traveling without a support person, I had carefully planned everything I needed to carry by myself while I was there – including Jane. I was able to pack successfully, by bringing the minimal needs for me in order to be comfortable, yet practical, for the eight days. While it was an admitted challenge, I managed with:

- *A large duffle bag on wheels for all clothes;*
- *A backpack (which served as a travel diaper bag with all her "baby care" needs) – we were unsure if there would be a store there to buy baby items – it turned out there was, but it was one less thing to worry about while there;*
- *A "snugli" front baby carrier (if winter, make sure a snow suit with "legs" vs. a "drawstring style" is used);*
- *A briefcase with a shoulder strap to hold all documents, papers, and travel information.*

I had one free hand* to support the baby as I pulled the large duffle bag with the other. My passport and money ($7,000 cash) were in a money belt around my waist beneath my wind suit.

In preparation for the physical and emotional rigors of travel in China as well as the long flights, I exercised at the down town Memphis YMCA to build up my endurance and conditioning. I was able to incorporate this into a regular routine before work. In retrospect, it definitely made the trip much more tolerable.

Reflection

*It is interesting to compare of my "modern age" maneuvering with a now retired statue by Lladro called "My Precious Bundle." It depicts a Chinese mother with a basket type back carrier looking lovingly over her shoulder with one free hand (symbolically similar to my free hand) tucked behind her back to ensure that her "cargo" was safe.

Coping Mechanisms

• Constant prayer – the basis of our spirituality

• Inspirational verses, sayings, and readings to keep our minds and hearts positive and "right" with God

• Past religious retreat material and reflections on information and decision-making frameworks obtained and absorbed while on retreats

• Discussion with adoption agencies and other "adoptive parents" to ensure that we were doing everything we could

• Internet information – presently, readily available. A wonderful comprehensive resource not as available in the mid 1990's

• Family discussions – immediate/extended for encouragement

• Friends (though several still seemed tentative about our decision – it just did not make sense, on the surface, to them)

• Timeliness and thoroughness of task completion – it gave us a feeling of some control through an active involvement in managing the process and that we had done everything possible toward the goal of adoption

• Visible symbolism to remind us of God's support and direction. In particular, lighthouses are favorites as they represent the illumination God sends to us on following straight and desired paths – especially in time of need and darkness!

Home Visit

The home visit, about which we were very nervous, turned out to be very routine. Between Kathy and me, we had been responsible for many licensing and accrediting "inspections" during our military and work careers. However, we felt very anxious about this review. We were told that a major component of the assessment would be out ability to manage a household budget and ensure that the environment was safe, loving and clean. (In retrospect, I did not need to be out in the yard at 11:30 p.m. the evening before spreading mulch in the garden!) The children were placed on notice and "the fear of God" lecture was delivered (to the children) for their best behavior. When my son responded "not really" to the question — "Are you excited about a new baby sister," I am sure that both Kathy and I stopped breathing momentarily. Unfazed, Janet Lawrence volleyed back — "I'll bet you prefer a little brother." Jonathan chimed in a definite "yes." Janet laughed and said "He's normal" and moved on with the study. (The advice is: be prepared but be yourselves!)

Reflection —Travel

Many people, as they grow older, have an increased tendency of wanting to stay at home in favor of experiencing long-distance travel. We are surrounded by the familiarity of friends, routine hobbies and occupations.

However, with age and maturity, there also comes the wisdom and understanding that we want to realize some of the objectives we have worked for throughout our lives. We seek to promote a better understanding among diverse peoples both locally and globally; and, to make a difference in the communities in which we live. Some of us are called to fulfill a global apostolic need, which may require long distance travel outside our comfort zone. Some people, by nature, will always thirst for new knowledge and therefore embrace the ex-citement of travel. (Rockwell, 1977)

I think in life we all have a tendency to become complacent with what we are doing. It truly wasn't comfortable for me to have my current work tasks smoothly transitioned and covered; leave my family; incur the expense of traveling over to China to pick up this child in a communist country, and, feel good about it! Scripture offers confidence and reassurance for safe travel. "I carried you away on eagles' wings and brought you to me." (Exodus 19:4) In many ways, it would have been easier to select a child from another country and receive the child as he or she got off the plane. This is not a criticism of countries in which this is the cultural adoptive practice. However, in retrospect, I think it was extremely useful and beneficial for me to witness, first hand, the environment Jane came from. This increased my awareness of and sensitivity to the Chinese people, their nuances, characteristic differences, and helped me to better understand their views on human rights. We all have the opportunity to experience adventure and enrich our hearts and minds through prayer to fulfill God's expectations.

Note: In late 1995, the adoption process took five months. Currently, the waiting time approximates 11 to 12 months from application start to travel and requires a 12 to a 16-day trip. This extended travel time incorporates several days of tourism and further acquaintance with China's culture. Again, as I speak, changes are occurring to improve the process based on comments from those who have gone before.

Reflection

There are instances along life's journey where we have felt vulnerable and unsure of ourselves. Oftentimes, these situations are related to the uncertainty of new and unusual surroundings, feelings of threat from others, lack of an ability to "control situations"; and, anxiety when we feel we might not be able to achieve all our dreams, meet needs, and fulfill responsibilities. In times of physical or emotional fear, we invoke prayer for protection and safety through difficult journeys.

Several relevant scriptural reflections follow:

• *"You alone, O Lord, make me dwell in safety." (Psalm 4:8)*

• *"In the dwelling of your presence you hid them from the intrigues of men, in your dwelling you keep them safe." (Psalm 31:20)*

• *"He will command His angels, concerning you, to guard you carefully." (Psalm 91:11-12)*

• *"For the Lord watches over the plans and paths of godly men." (Psalm 1:6)*

• *"Do not be afraid, nor be dismayed, be strong and of good courage, for thus the Lord will do." (Joshua 10:25)*

• *"Living or dying we follow the Lord. Either way we are his." (Romans 14:8)*

A Father's Journal

As we mentioned earlier, I made a conscious effort to capture the reflections of my trip along with observations and feelings in a journal. Kathy, our families, and friends directed that I not spare a detail. They were eager to absorb the chronology of every encounter!

Unknowingly, the inclusion of my emotions in the journal captured what I term a "transformation" or "a conversion experience." So, in addition to the (intended) "how" of the process, in retrospect, my journal more fully illuminated the methodical reasons "why" we adopted.

Reflection

As a result of our adoption, I realized that this "conversion experience" was life-changing so that I would never be the same again. "Conversion" often times infers a change in one's religious faith. I did not change religions; nor was this a sudden conversion (like the Biblical Paul experienced.) Rather, mine was a gradual inner conversion guided by maturity — nurtured with a combination of increased awareness of process dynamics and my personal spiritual growth. I did, however, express what I would term "instantaneous realization" during my journey. This was more like the common mini-phenomenon I'm sure we all experience when "the light bulb goes on" and "we get it."

Journal

January 26, 1996 — Friday

0500 – Memphis, Tennessee…Woke up and got ready to travel to airport…Katie and Jonathan came with Kathy to bid me farewell, along with Janet Lawrence, Director, Mid-South Christian Services. This morning before we left for the airport, we decided on the name Jane Su Rudnick. While nervous about my travel, Kathy and the children looked forward to my return next week. I have the Rosary (prayer beads) of Patrick King lent to me by his parents, John and Barbara, close friends (Patrick died last year at age 5)…I am still amazed at the selfless generosity of John and Barbara to part with such a treasured possession.

0810 – Left Memphis for first stop, Chicago.

1030 – Arrive Chicago.

1145 – Went to the Chicago airport chapel to pray for a safe trip, good health for all concerned – especially the babies - and a successful process.

1230 – Travel to Tokyo – 12 hours; drinking lots of water; two full movies have helped to pass the time.

1820 – Layover in Tokyo…3.5 hour flight to Shanghai lies ahead; met up with other parties in group; all seem nice.

2100 – Slept most of the way – glad we are here; while the travel pillow helps, I have a stiff neck.

2100 – Arrive, Shanghai – a bit confusing; airport appearance is reminiscent of a 1960's European style building – stark, simple, clean.

Country entrance processing included clearance for health (called quarantine), and immigration (passport verification) before locating luggage. Observations: Very crowded, older city; many bright neon signs; streets were congested at 9:30 p.m. on a Saturday with cars, taxis, and people on bicycles. Bicyclists weave their way throughout traffic and cars at alarming closeness.

People, for the most part, move quickly and precisely.

Called Kathy and the kids to check on Katie's cold; and, to wish Jonathan luck with the (Cub Scout) Pinewood Derby – the first I have ever missed.

The money currency is "Yuan"…unlike most U.S. currency, the smaller coins represent more. The exchange rate is eight yuan to 1 U.S. dollar.

Tipping seems awkward. I used an American standard of $1 per bag for the bellman.

January 28, 1996 — Sunday

Got up early, milled around the hotel, did a brief workout in the exercise room and ate breakfast (many appealing choices on hotel buffet). Sat out in lobby while waiting for others in the group and walked outside around the hotel. For a Sunday, it appears to be a regular workday.

1200 – Left for Shanghai airport for trip to Changsha; airport very crowded – security somewhat lax by comparison to our U.S. standards; people were slightly pushing and jockeying for position while in line for the ticket counters.

Children dress in bright primary colors; adults dress in drab olives and browns; styles are similar to ours…men's suits do not have tags removed from outside of sleeves in many cases!

Still drinking lots of water.

1230- 1730 – Layover and delay in Shanghai airport due to "aircraft turnover." Caught a quick nap…waiting is tiring…played cards to pass the time. Flight packed – seats small.

Bags were not stowed away – people were moving about the cabin during takeoff…seemed a bit chaotic by our standards – but the pilots were determined to go when they decided they were ready!

1900 – Arrived at Changsha airport – large airfield, overwhelming activity, very old terminal — small; the tarmac was very busy with 7-8 huge aircraft with hundreds of people disembarking simultaneously...we all walked (on the tarmac) toward a small terminal building to get our luggage. We were still without interpreter assistance – this is where we were to meet June…but did not see her right away – 15 minutes seemed like an eternity in this foreign land and a packed building with curious people stopping and staring. June finally spotted us just after we had already located our luggage.

22-mile ride to hotel…rural countryside terrain…homes do not appear to have electricity (no visible wires) and all had candlelight for light visible from the windows in the cement huts which seemed in the middle of expansive fields (as seen from the headlights of the van).

Hotel arrival at 2030…ate in Chinese Restaurant after check-in.

0730 – Watched some of Super Bowl XXX in my room …international television stations are broadcast there on a limited basis…it brought good memories of "home."

1000 - Traveled to a cross-town hotel to begin the process to complete the physical exchange of the infants which would take place early this afternoon…the process seems fragmented and inefficient by our standards, but you learn to roll with the flow. There were six people from the agency in the room where we were brought back two at a time…the lead person was young, had a pair of glasses with one cracked lens, spoke fluent, unbroken English fairly proficiently, and was all business. He reviewed information from the home study that had been sent to China from the agency; and from the duplicate requested from us while we were there (It was clear that there was a good bit of overlap and redundancy.)

There were several points that we needed to commit to on the document we were asked to sign:

• We would obtain a certificate during our stay, for our baby, from the Health Department; and, obtain necessary certified documents for the notary in order to complete the adoption paperwork.

• We would travel to the Civil Affairs Office on the other side of town to complete this.

• We must provide a copy of the home study to any of the agencies that requested a duplicate copy.

• We must promise that we will never abuse, abandon, harm, hit (our baby), or give her up for adoption.

• We must obey the rules while in China.

• We will pay a donation to the orphanage as had been previously stipulated by the agency prior to coming to China.

My heart melted when I saw the small black and white referral photo (the same one as the one that had been sent to us) affixed to the top of one of the documents.

The interviewer wanted to know why we wanted a Chinese baby – especially in light of the fact that we already had two children of our own at home. My response was that we were responding to the need we had heard about and strongly felt called to take action to help. We love children and thought this would be a wonderful addition to our family. He accepted this matter of factly, and moved on with the process.

Again, we had to promise that we would never abandon her.

I was given a booklet (similar to a "Blue Book" in which I took many of my college examinations and tests) and asked to respond in writing to the following:
• Why we wanted to adopt Su Qing and that we would comply with the items previously discussed in the interview.
• We needed to profile personal data about ourselves and our family.
• We had to affix our thumb-print at the end of the essay with red ink. We were then handed a roll of toilet paper to wipe the ink from our thumb.
• We then paid a $150 registration fee there.
After we finished the registration process there, we hopped into two taxis and fought traffic for about 25 minutes through the crowded streets and winding alleys en route to another part of town to meet with the notary.
1130 – The electricity went off just as we arrived — we did virtually all our paperwork by candlelight. (The burning candle reminds me of the Easter vigil candle our church congregation lights from the Easter candle in preparation for celebrating the resurrection of Jesus Christ. Certainly, it seemed that Jane would have suffered through a passion, of sorts, as she lay in a crib.) We were informed there – (somewhat repetitiously) that, by Chinese law, we needed to be aware of and compliant with several items; we will take care of her; and give her a good education.

…Back to the hotel to get things ready to go to the orphanage …excitement is growing as we get ready to go – estimated time of departure – 1430. Note: The hotel generator was frequently shut down so that electricity outages occurred sporadically—usually for no more than 60-90 minutes once or twice a day while in Changsha.

Orphanage, Changsha, China–1996

1430 – Trip to orphanage takes about 20 minutes. June rented a van large enough to accommodate bringing the babies home with us. Along the way, we saw the typical day in the lives of the people of Changsha. There were open markets with raw meat hanging off wooden racks made from tree limbs and wooden shelves containing fruits, vegetables, and cigarettes. Young girls, appearing to be 13-14 years old, sat on the curbstone (10-12 in an area) with a stool and shoe shine-kits waiting for work. Everyone here seems fast and on the run.

Steve (Shaner) and I remarked at the positive, eager, conscientious work ethic among people here – both by observation in the streets and here at the hotel. We turned up a drive sandwiched between two columns and two "strip malls" of businesses. All in the van, except June, were totally absorbed with the buildings and the surroundings. I sensed there must be older children here at the orphanage as there was a basketball hoop near the side of the concrete driveway…this made me a bit sad (i.e., that older children would be here as they most likely have poor adoption prospects. We were told that the older children have special needs.) We took several pictures, ran the camcorder, and proceeded into the building behind June.

Because we were told that this was one of the better orphanages, we expected something different and better from the physical plant appearances. The important thing at this point was our concern that the babies were in good hands and well cared for – the stairwells were not cleaned very well and the marble steps were worn in two semicircles where most of the walking traffic took place. The second floor was red and worn…there were rings of dirt, standing water puddled in the low spots on the floor – just enough for a reflection — and in the bathroom as well. The windows in the halls and the bathrooms were wide open with no screens. There were white ceramic spittoons outside each door – for trash and cigarette butts I observed in them. We were only allowed to go one third of the way down the hall and went left into the room where we were to pick up the children. I labeled it the "adoption room."

There was heat in this room unlike the hall, stairwell, and bathroom. Security bars were in place on the windows inside and outside. The hall walls, which rose to 12-14 foot ceilings, were light green and somewhat soiled with dirt marks.

As we walked into the adoption room, it was a surprise to see the four babies, to our right, being held by the orphanage attendants. There were seven administrative people there – attendants and the gentleman with the cracked glasses from the hotel earlier that morning. There were heavy black vinyl chairs on commercial rust and scarlet shag carpet.

A large oval table in the middle resembling a casino table with a pit in the middle resembling a craps table in the center.

We all went to the sides and back of the room waiting to be told what to do. I assessed the babies carefully and nervously thought— I do not recognize Jane.

Then I heard the attendants say something and started shifting around in their chairs as if they wanted something to happen. I said

"Su Qing(Ching) she said - - Su Qing and rose with a baby swaddled in four layers of clothing and a blue polka-dot snow suit.

The first thing I noticed was her shaved head. I picked her up slowly, looked briefly at Jane's face, and held her close to me and walked slowly around the room. The other families were getting acquainted with their babies. There were tears and laughter and an overall feeling of happiness.

Jane had bright red flushed cheeks. Her eyes seemed glazed and her head flopped left and right. From that point on I held her head with my fingers. The side of her head looked bruised. (This turned out to be partially her skin color and bruising from injections probably being given into head for her bronchitis as there were pinpoint scabs near the sides of her temples). A long scratch on the side of her face signaled possible long nails. Sure enough, they were long and pointed - - they looked like miniature adult nails. After a few moments with pictures, the staff went around and collected their snow suits.

A middle-aged, heavyset attendant, very happy, patted the babies. She was genuinely sad but happy as she patted Jane. It was odd - - I somehow had the feeling I had seen that attendant before. Probably resembled someone back home! I thanked her, through the interpreter, for taking care of Jane. We asked if they knew anything about their backgrounds and if we could see where they stayed. We were told that they knew nothing of these caldrons backgrounds and that visitation in other

Jane with orphanage caretaker– "Adoption Day," January 29, 1996

parts of the orphanage was not allowed. We returned to the vans for a hair-raising ride back to the hotel with many bumps and jolts - - no seat belts or car seats available - - us all held the babies tight to us! We seemed to be fulfilling a need at that moment captured in this verse: "Save us, Lord, our God. Gather us from among the nations …" (Psalms 106:47)

Reflection

I did not witness anything but care and concern for the babies in our group — from the time we arrived at the orphanage until we boarded the plane to leave. "…blest are your eyes because they see…" (Matt. 13:16). The conditions at the orphanage were poor by comparison to American standards. However, there are so many orphans in China and resources are so limited that it seems that they do the best they can with what they have. Certainly, the babies we brought back were better cared for in a government orphanage there as compared with "life on the streets." Like the maternal nature and roles played by the woman of Jerusalem, the infants were blessed with the support of a group of Chinese women assigned by the government to do the best they could for them in the orphanage with the resources they had. (These women were probably unaware that they were fulfilling a basic need with strong Biblical significance — "I was hungry and you gave me food…") (Matt. 26:35,45)

Reflection – Missions

My observation while in China ran a broad gamut of emotions. What I quickly realized is that the culture and values embraced by other countries are vastly different. We are all called to know our Lord by honoring Him through service to others whom we encounter in our earthly life. Some of us are called to use our gifts and talents close to home. Others are called to a more global apostolic ministry for helping other countries. While we typically think of "missions" as being in overseas, undeveloped countries, some "mission" trips are made to help the poor in domestic communities. People living in impoverished circumstances who are not exposed to the benefit of communication with the "outside" world may well have no awareness or knowledge of human rights values consistent with scriptural teachings relative to such issues as abortion, infanticide, or euthanasia as many of us who have been privileged to hear. There-fore, it is our responsibility to build up God's Kingdom here on earth and help promote the value of "life" through prayer, devotion of time, material resources, and/or direct service which can take place in a variety of forms. Inspiring Scriptural messages about missions include the following:

• *"And now,…He is sending us around the world to tell all people everywhere the great things God has done for them, so that they, too, will believe and obey Him." (Romans 1:5)*

• *"Make most of your chances to tell others the good news. Be wise in all your contacts with them." (Colossians 4:5)*

• *"You are to go into the world and preach the Good News to everyone, everywhere." (Mark 16:15)*

• *"The harvest is plentiful but the workers are few. Ask the Lord of the harvest, therefore, to send out workers into his harvest fields." (Matt. 9:37-38)*

• *"I have heard the message from the Lord; He has sent a mes-senger to call the nations." (Jeremiah 49:14)*

• *"As God's partners, we beg you not to toss aside this marvelous message of God's great kindness." (2 Corinth. 6:1)*

• *"Look around you, vast fields of human souls are re-penting all around us, and are ready now for reaping." (John 4:35)*

• *"Honor all people." (I Peter 2:17)*

• *"He appointed the priests to their duties and encouraged them in the service of the Lord's temple." (2 Chronicles 35:2)*

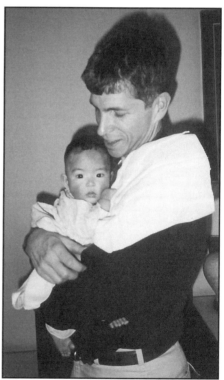

Jane in dad's arms

Continued missionary work and advances in communication will hopefully have a positive effect on how future generations, especially in overseas countries, respond to human rights issues. Again, there are many domestic opportunities for us to witness to (human rights issues) here in the United States.

Jane was very good throughout the afternoon. She adapted to the bottle and formula right away. Her cough and stuffiness in the later evening proved a bit uncomfortable. After a crying spell, (probable pain was from an ear infection), Pediasure, and Amoxicillin we fell asleep about 3:30 a.m. Debby Shaner came over from their room and helped me get Jane calmed down. We had done about four 15-minute steam shower visits in an attempt to loosen the tightness in her chest. We awoke rested at about 9:00 a.m. June came and helped me bathe Jane. June shared that the babies received the equivalent of one sponge bath weekly. Jane had dirt and dead skin caked in between her fingers and toes, resembling webbed hands and feet. (Christ uses water as a powerful symbol. He set an example for us to follow: "…he poured water into the basin and washed (their) feet…and dried them with the towel…") (John 13:17). I had to take and manually define each finger and toe. Jane also had a minor diaper rash. As is often the case with Asian children, she had a "Mongolian Birthmark" on her back. We were told that, oftentimes, these fade as the children get older (however, we had been advised that we need to document this with our pediatrician as these marks which look like bruises could be mistaken as bruises and be a sign of potential child abuse if seen by an uninformed observer). She did not like her first bath at all. June calmed her down…this was about 11:30 a.m. I put Jane down…she slept from 12-3:30. Some upper respiratory infection is probable. Pat, a nurse and one of the companions on the trip, helped with percussion treatments to loosen the cough and deep-set cold.

Reflection
When I first got Jane, she was well cared for, but had dirt and sores in the folds of her tiny skin. There were just too many babies and far too little staff and resources to fully address all hygiene and medical needs. The Biblical story of the beggar, Lazarus, with his sores, and the example of Jesus (and the current Pope, John Paul II

and the late Mother Teresa) are among notable figures, because of their focus, practices, and philosophy. They exemplified service to the poor and less fortunate. The washing of the feet of men and women (John 13:1-17) also witnesses to the privilege of being entrusted to care for these people as Christ would expect.

1600-1800 – Shopped with June and several members of the group while two of the ladies took their turn watching the babies...we agreed to trade off sitting for these short shopping sprees.

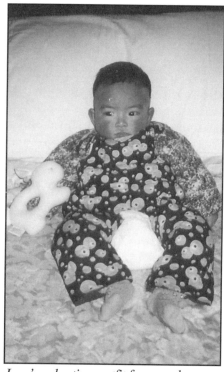

Jane's adoption outfit from orphanage

The stores are somewhat reminiscent of (department stores in) the late 50s, 60s in terms of the decor, products, mannequins, maroon and gold uniforms of the staff, and the use of an abacus on the counter and a cardboard box on the floor to process cash transactions.

Bought several gifts for relatives and friends back home. There are many bargains by comparison to similar items in the U.S. The handstitched silk, jade, and pictures were especially reasonable. Looked at jade pigs (year of Jane's birth)...Will buy tomorrow when there is more time to browse.

June shared that babies are typically left in public places for people to find them and deliver them to the police station, where a record is prepared, then they are taken to a government-run orphanage.

Called Kathy to let her know that all was well and that Jane was perking up and developing a personality.

Dinner at the Marco Polo Restaurant in the other of the hotel's three dining areas.

Called Janet Lawrence and Shiyan Zeng in the United States as we had questions about some of the paperwork and process...all was deemed to be in order. Jane had a rough night. We were up until 4:30 a.m. She seemed happy and cooed from 2:30-3:30.

Woke up at 8:30 a.m....lounged around in the morning...breakfast of instant oatmeal using the boiled hot water available on each floor from the concierge. All going well.

Bought several towels for the orphanage for the babies there to have clean adequate towels when they are given baths; and gave them a sleeper of Jane's and one of the blankets I had brought along.

1330 – Shopped for several gift items for friends at home and small wrapped "penny candy" for us to distribute to the children's classmates and our friends in the neighborhood, work, and church.

Incident at the department store...while shopping, we were approached by Chinese-man and woman. She stood behind and watched...he had front teeth missing...he wanted to have us exchange money with him for more than better exchange rate than at the department store. We quickly declined and left as we had no interest in this and did not know what could be construed in a Communist country, even if we were just seen talking with them.

June directed us to buy tickets from Changsha to Guangzhou for US cost was $77.50 plus an additional 25 percent more "for the baby." We are to verify the flights and confirm 72 hours in advance of travel. We were advised to fax confirmation of our arrival to the White Swan Hotel for reconfirmation of those reservations and to request airport pick-up.

Just before turning in for the night, we received our final paperwork for travel to Guangzhou.

Found out that the original date given for Jane's birth (August 4) was in error...the actual date, according to both police and orphanage records, is July 4, 1995.

The assistant duty manager at the hotel pointed out on a map where Jane was abandoned. It was in rural Changsha about 20 min-

Estimated vicinity of abandonment

utes from the center of town…based on our limited experiences with driving around the area, there was probably no electricity where she was born in this poor community. Her home was probably in a cement hut with four apartments on two floors, based on the typical design of most of the buildings we observed through the countryside.

Phone bill from hotel very high. MCI does not service China due to past abuses of the overseas service. It may be worth getting an alternative if MCI does not service this when people travel.

Chinese girls very pretty. Most are slender and fair…the red lipstick with the black hair and fair complexion is a striking combination of beauty. Jane slept from the hotel to the airport. The "snugli" I used to carry her in front of me was very useful…she does, however, get heavy after an hour!

There was no heat at the airport…very cold…much nicer, however, and less hectic than Shanghai. Countryside of Changsha in outskirts reminds me of the cranberry bogs in Cape Cod where I spent summers and is now the home of my parents. The rice fields and huge community gardens frame the highways on both sides.

February 1, 1996 – Friday

Boarded flight for our next leg of the journey. Flight was relatively short and smooth. Picture made with flight attendant.

Arrived at the White Swan; Guangzhou is a strikingly brighter city and a bit more uplifting than Changsha…Perhaps this was because it was the first real sunlit day since we had arrived. The colors here are very bright as opposed to the pearlish gray pallor that hovered over Changsha. The taxi ride from the airport to the White Swan was also hair-raising. It is a bustling city with pedestrians, vehicles, and bicycles *very* co-mingled in the streets.

The White Swan is one of the nicest hotels I have ever been in. The room has a breathtaking view of the city and canal which hosts a variety of boats, barges, and Vietnam-style dories on the Pearl River. The men and women wear large round straw hats.

I had a real surprise when I checked into the hotel and discovered that I had a message from a friend, Patrick Lappert, who had relocated from Memphis to Virginia two years earlier…at Christmas, a year ago they had written that they were traveling to China in March 1995 to pick up their new daughter…so, I was taken aback to learn he was there. His 82-year-old mother-in-law, Mary Oberst, accompanied him there. I later learned that for personal reasons they

Jane and dad boarding Chinese aircraft for first ride.

70

had to delay their trip which worked out well for them...and us!

It was a hectic check-in as we had to immediately go downstairs to get airline tickets for Hong Kong. The room has a king-size bed and refrigerator...the amenities are superb. After we got settled, we fed the babies and walked to the clinic for the children's exit medical exam and to obtain passport photos.

Friends Debbie and Steve Shaner with Katelyn.

Jane is 5.5 kg and 63.5 cm long. The examining doctor did not think she had good breathing sounds. When we got to the clinic, she was upset and croupy.

The doctor there said she was very sick and that I needed to consider bringing her to another doctor for some medicine. I felt uneasy about taking her just anywhere, so I decided to go back to the hotel to think and pray. Then I remembered Patrick, a physician! I phoned him — he volunteered that he had brought a stethoscope and a bag of antibiotics and would be glad to take a look at her...he determined that she was fine, with some minor superficial infections which would be taken care of with the Augmentin he had brought along.

"Those who are well do not need a physician, but the sick do." (Matt. 9:12)

Rita, their two-year-old, is very cute and has a bubbly personality. Patrick needs to remain a few more days as their airplane to Virginia was delayed. The airline they flew on only travels once a week and they could not get tickets back early. He told us where there was a church to visit in the city and recommended that we visit there.

It was a wonderful feeling to be in a nice hotel...tea was served upon request with an in-room pot complete with a tea cozie. I sat

71

with my feet propped up, feeding Jane, drinking tea, watching the boats go by from the fourteenth floor of the hotel...it doesn't get much better.

February 1, 1996 – Friday

Baby up until 2:30 a.m., ear infection probable as crying is intense and she is tugging on her ears...this is frustrating as I feel badly for her...while it definitely helped, the Augmentin, even though given regularly, does not seem to be fully doing the trick.

Boarded plane to Guangzhou...good flight...Jane slept most of the way...picture made with flight attendant.

Chinese planes were very old...service very good...responsive flight attendants. Fewer safety restrictions. Jane smiling a lot. Gurgles and coos as she discovers her voice. Loves to be sung to...

Jane with dad en route to Guangzhou (formerly Canton), China.

6:30 a.m....Got up to get ready. The infant Moses' basket was perfect for the baby sleeping at night and carrying her to some of the other hotel rooms to be watched.

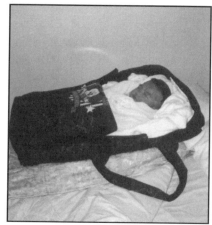

Jane in "Moses Basket"

The staff at the hotel really made over the babies. Again, most young adults showed genuine affection for the babies as we walked through the hotel.

Group photos at the airport.

I averaged 3-4 hours of sleep/ day or night...I can catch up when I get back to the U.S.

Reflection

Upon reflection, it seems that with the number of babies there to be adopted (about 500,000 in 1996 – now in 2000 hovering 800,000 to 1,000,000) it is clear that couples or singles who want children have an opportunity to satisfy this, a mutual need, between adoptive parents and China.

Prominent futurist Dr. Leland Kaiser once said that when children are going hungry and lack immunizations in communities near business and industry where the company is turning handsome profits and do nothing to help solve social ills, these companies are committing a crime against humanity. "If anyone has possessions and sees his brother in need but has no pity on him, how can the love of God be in him?" (1John 3:17) I feel fortunate and good about our decision to tap our 403(b) tax-sheltered annuity and being able to take advantage of the no-penalty loan provision to get started with this process.

Fifty babies were processed through the consulate while we were there on Thursday – the day where those who adopt from south-central China come to process the paperwork for completing and finalizing the adoption process; and, bringing necessary paperwork to the U.S. (We were given envelopes not to be opened and were told to hand to immigration officers when we arrived in Los Angeles, California.)

The Chinese young adult women, again, are respectful and cleanly groomed. They all make over the babies in a genuine and caring way. Jane will grow up to be striking, I predict, with her jet black shiny hair, fair complexion, and deep dark eyes (June, the interpreter referred to them as black eyes...I shared with June that black eye has a different meaning in the U.S.!) Jane's eyes are a perfect almond shape when open...when closed they resemble a button hole slit. Her bottom lashes sometimes mat against her eyes.

Jane loves to be placed high in the air and gently shaken from side to side. She prefers to have her head held up and is not happy lying flat on either her back or her stomach. I think she is frustrated that she cannot push herself up or roll over. Her head control is slowly improving daily. I have been having her curl her hands around my fingers and pull her up to strengthen her neck muscles. She is beginning to recognize her name.

The name Su Qing is significant from several perspectives. Su, her Chinese surname is typically one given to all in this particular orphanage. Su Qing, together, translates to "clean and white." When she was found, she was given this name because she was clean, well cared for, and had a fair complexion.

The reason that there are dates associated with Jane's background relates to the cultural ritual of abandonment. A piece of paper and string was looped around her neck with nothing but her birth date

Usually babies are abandoned 1-2 days after birth. Greg Haskel, American Consulate, discussed the likely scenario with this type of abandonment – that the birth-mother wanted to keep Jane, but probably relented to pressure from the husband or mother-in-law.

Reflection

We need to pray that the birth mother finds comfort with this loss. (Recall the pain that Mary and Joseph – mother and foster father of Jesus – felt with the three-day separation from Jesus, then finally located him teaching in the temple. They were alarmed and concerned with no knowledge of his whereabouts.) What a struggle to part with this special gift.

Jane cries when getting her diaper changed without first propping her head up on a pillow. She loves her "Nuk" pacifier. (Baby items can be bought in the department stores.) Jane's appetite is good. She seemed to eat more during the first part of the week. Now she seems to require less.

She is the oldest of the group but seems like the "runt of the litter" in terms of size and development. Everyone remarks how beautiful her hair is and her stunning features. She is a wonderful traveler.

A discussion with the director of the medical clinic proved interesting. All Chinese have access to health care with a socialized medical system. They want to move more toward delivering healthcare with insurance products similar to what we have in the United States. The radiology fluoroscopy room seemed to be a 1950s vintage. The room was not very clean – there were exposed wires at the base of the unit.

I obtained a copy of the newspaper (in English) for the day we received Jane. I took stationery and bought other mementos to share with Jane as she gets older.

We were able to get along without the interpreter for almost half of the trip but felt as though, language wise, we were in the "Tower of Babel" with people speaking different languages.

The Chinese revere their elderly…senior citizens were participating in Tai Chi movement in the parks around the hotel. The Chinese have a diet focusing on fruits, vegetables, grains and seafood.

With regard to the existence of religion, June shared that more and more young people are beginning to practice Christianity.

As far as the values system and the manner in which the Chinese deal with the population challenges, I contend that because of the "closed communication loop and influences of the Government" on how they live, their outlook and the way they handle issues cannot be totally criticized. They do not know differently.

As we walk around and young adults stop us about every two blocks to make over the babies and say "...Lucky girl"...one has to wonder if in the U.S., children are as taken or realize their good fortune. Young adults admiring children in the U.S. do not seem as prevalent...it is obvious, however, that the admirers know why we are here and realize that the babies are going on to a better life.

Note: The Journal ends here as we are about to embark on a 30-hour trip home. I can't wait to see Kathy and the children...

Jane, I hope this captures all that I know what little we know about your background and how you came to us. You will always be such a precious blessing to us. I love you, Dad.

Coincidence

(Elaboration of Journal entry)

Our U.S. Navy veteran status prompted a commonality with friends Patrick and Patrice Lappert when we both lived in Memphis, Tennessee during a three-year period. Patrick and his wife Patrice had moved away to Virginia two years before we decided to adopt. Through the exchange of Christmas cards, we shared our intent, as they did, to adopt a child from China. However, they were 6-9 months ahead of us in the processing cycle. What we did not know was that a personal reason – a family member's surgery – forced the delay of their trip. When I got to China, surprisingly, I had a message that Patrick was staying at the same hotel as me due to a delay in his flight leaving China.

During the exit physical for Jane, I was told she needed medical attention for her bronchitis. Not knowing where to turn, you can imagine my surprise that Patrick, a physician, was at my same hotel at the same time. My wife, Kathy, had called Patrice – who also had remained home to care for her children – like Kathy – to share the excitement and prospect of my travel, pending my return home, and just to catch up. It proved to be a providential call. Patrice had called and told Patrick I was scheduled to be there and he contacted me. He had a stethoscope and a more potent antibiotic to help sustain and help Jane until we could get back to the United States.

Reflection

God certainly did come through and caringly provided for us. The faith, trust, and confidence we had learned through our life experiences helped me through this difficult event in our journey. Prayer and patience helped sustain us. A focus on wanting to do what is right and fulfill God's will for us leads us to His intended direction for us. Religion and spirituality are important in our lives. We may not realize until later in life how a "chance meeting" or "encounter" can have such a tremendous and awesome effect on us!

Reflection — Safety/Protection

The following verses illustrate the reinforcement that God continuously watches over us:

- *"You have given me your salvation as my shield..." (Psalm 18:35)*
- *"Blessed is the Lord, for He has shown me that His never-failing love protects me like the walls of a fort!" (Psalm 31:21)*
- *"Watch your step, steer to the path and be safe." (Proverbs 4:26)*
- *"Be strong and courageous. Do not be terrified; do not be discouraged, for the Lord your God will be with you wherever you go." (Joshua 1:9)*

Return From China / Airport Reunion

"Anyone who welcomes a little child welcomes me" (Mark 9:37).

The exhaustion we felt during our plane ride home from China was mixed with my anticipation of seeing Kathy, Katie, Jonathan and our family/friends. I was fortunate that "well-wishers" on our flight offered to hold and care for Jane so that I could eat and rest a bit. The airline flight attendants showed genuine interest and care for us throughout the trip. The thirty hours of travel was broken up nicely with a layover in Chicago. Our good friends, Bill and Judi Schanelic, braved the winter cold to meet us at the airport during our layover. They shared our excitement as the first Americans to meet Jane and Katelyn Shaner. Adrenaline kept me alert and eager during the last leg of the journey. When I stepped off the plane onto the jetway in Memphis, I had Jane wrapped in my winter jacket, as it was bitter cold. After walking up the ramp to the terminal, I

Kathy anxiously awaits Jane's airport arrival.

was greeted with blinding flashbulbs from clicking cameras. The next thing I recall was embracing Kathy and placing Jane into her arms. I was also eager to see Katie and Jonathan. In the chaos, everyone enjoyed the balloons, cheers, and tears of other family members and friends.

When my luggage was not in the baggage claim area, I recalled the conditions in China. My outlook on this issue became "all relative." The five of us drove home for our first night together! The bags all arrived and were delivered 10 hours later the next morning!

Advice – Expectations/Considerations

• Do select an agency that is reputable, accessible, friendly, and suited to your personality and overall needs. Address staff openness to receiving frequent contact for clarification and updates. Determine mutually expedient communication preferences (i.e., phone, e-mail, faxes, letter).

• Do talk with appropriate sources and obtain as much information as is needed to make an informed decision.

• Do not force or reach a decision based on emotion without feeling fully comfortable with all aspects – objective and subjective.

• Do consider the effects on your entire immediate family. Assess their emotional readiness and involve them in all the appropriate planning aspects (including money, where the new child will sleep, and other miscellaneous logistics).

• Do not take information gleaned from the internet solely as

The Rudnick's first family picture together.

"God's gospel" without adequate verification with your agency (or, if initially inquiring, an appropriate agency).

• Do verify question, concerns, and information verification you may have with adoption agency contacts.

• Do attend adoption meetings and reunions for information about adoption; and, get a feel for how adoptive families interact with their children. Expect to find happy, helpful, and congenial attendees.

• Do discuss the "risk tolerance" you have both within your family, as appropriate, and with the agency as there is a risk, albeit calculated, on the health and temperament of children adopted overseas. Be reminded, however, of the potential for health risks for "biological children" as well.

• Do participate in church and spiritual events for support. Remember to pray for what you need and be thankful for what you receive.

• Do beware of projecting too many disadvantages on what might happen.

• Do not base your decision on someone else's approval or to please someone else. (i.e., spouse, family members, friends). As an individual *you* must be comfortable.

• Do rely and draw on past difficult experiences when encountering frustration or challenges with the process. Recall that you "got through" the past experience and it is likely that with time, additional information, patience, and prayer, you will probably get through this challenge successfully.

• Do avoid over-packing for yourself and the baby when traveling.

• Do ensure that you "dress down" – you do not want to draw further attention, especially in a foreign country.

• Do check in advance to determine if you can buy support needs for the child or you in the event that you forget something or don't want to carry some items (e.g. stroller).

• Do photocopy your passports, important papers, and itinerary. Leave copies with family or friends back in the United States as well as with the local adoption agency in the event of an emergency.

• Do maintain a detailed journal with the many occurrences of your trip. This will prove invaluable for you to share with your child and genuinely interested family and friends. Mine has proved to be a good source to consult years later when trying to recount or reconstruct part of the process. (Include detailed observations and feelings.)

• Do wear comfortable clothing when traveling as you will be carrying valuables – passports, cash, papers. Buy a "roller duffel."

• Do consider bringing or buying an umbrella stroller...especially if you know ahead of time that the child is more than 20 pounds!

• Do try to get in some good physical shape prior to the trip. Attend a local YMCA or health facility to get into a routine. Break in comfortable running/walking shoes. Good physical condition will contribute to a positive spirit and resiliency when fighting fatigue – especially during in-country travel and the trips to and from home.

• Do prepay as much as possible prior to travel to eliminate the need for cash. Try to find out if hotels where you will be staying accept major credit cards (and, if yes, which ones).

• Do consider bringing an empty small collapsible suitcase to bring home souvenirs and gifts. Buy special mementos for your adopted child for later in life to maintain his/her culture.

• Do not be outwardly judgmental of a foreign culture. You are a guest. Be analytical but withhold emotional opinions or criticism as to avoid unnecessary conflict. There are many frustrations and criticisms with process that we might not agree with or understand. Go with the flow to the extent possible for as smooth a process as possible. Keep focused on your overall goal.

• Do review, practice, and know something about the foreign currency, if possible, prior to going. Know the exchange rate. It may help prepare for the cash transactions to be made as well as checking the itemized expenses on the hotel bill. Consider bringing some currency for initial convenience.

• Do prepare yourself, if you travel, for bright lights, cheering, and tears when returning home. Be mindful that your new child is *scared* and entering a new culture and unfamiliar people. Try to maintain a close control over "passing the child off" to multiple friends and family as you meet the excitement and confusion. Relish the fantastic high of a mission accomplished and a job well done!

• Do be prepared for possible prejudice as you are now an "interracial" family. Talk to siblings regarding possible non-intentional slurs or remarks. Young children may need preparation and help with handling these situations.

• Do be open to talking with others who may be interested in the process. (What a compliment to you when someone finds your experiences fascinating.) Be humble, but don't be afraid to be proud and positive.

• Do pray for the courageous birth mother and father who chose to provide life and the option of adoption for your child so that the child would have a better life.

• Do be open to an objective test of your child's developmental factors relative to age. Four months of therapy and instruction made a tremendous difference for us. Be honest with pediatricians about concerns and fears about the child's development.

• Do not "sweat" the home study. Again, the agency wants to see if you offer a safe environment and practice good financial management in the household.

• Do drink water — especially while flying long distances to keep hydrated.

• Expect cultural nuances when traveling. Anticipate the need for "tipping." Obtain information on this (and care giver gift-giving) with your agency liaison.

• Expect systems and processes that, by our standards, may seem inefficient.

• Expect to function as a group when traveling. It may be useful to have a group meeting to assume various duties to help with the process. Issues include responsibility for: arranging in-country flights/ transportation; collecting money for group expenses...taxi, interpreter fees; verifying flight reservations and transportation throughout the stay. Anticipate the need for conflict resolution, compromise, trust building, flexibility and patience.

• Expect that you might not recognize your child right away. There may be changes from the time the original picture was taken. I recognized Jane because she was dressed in the same outfit as her picture!

• Expect stares from people. You are different! Also, most know why Americans are there and they, for the most part, admire the willingness of others to help their country.

• Expect the possibility of mistakes between the countries. Human error can occur on translation and simply information with the high volume of papers processed (i.e., we experienced a miscalculation on our child's age by one month).

• Expect an adjustment period if you are bringing a child into a house with a pet. It is very likely that the child has never interacted with a domestic pet (or other animal for that matter). Likewise, consider that the pet may need to adjust to a new household member. There may be jealousy and confusion. Be cautious about initial interaction.

• Expect possible changes in your circle of friends and patterns of interaction as your interests and circumstances change. Friends with whom you did certain activities may not have the interest or temperament to be around small children again.

• Expect some "stereo-type" remarks. With us being in "advanced middle age" it did almost seem like having a grandchild early. From a humorous perspective, I share this because of assumptions people make about children and age. Both Kathy and I experienced this with people's innocent observations – to Kathy: "Is Jane your only grandchild?" And to me: "I saw you at church Sunday with your family and beautiful granddaughter!"

Loyal friends with Kathy and Jane.

Reflections and Comments Specific to China

• Do bring $200-$500 extra cash for incidental processing expenses. Our group was asked to pay, as a group, an additional $500 "tax" for some clerical help to work overtime to get our paperwork ready for a tightly scheduled travel time frame.

• Expect crowds in public places in China. The pace seems more hectic and frenetic, with people behave with a sense of urgency.

• Expect conditions to possibly appear old, dated and tired-looking by U.S. standards — especially in the rural parts of China.

• Expect most hotels to carry traditional American foods, such as hamburgers and french fries.

• Expect crowds in country airline flights. Anticipate different boarding and disembarking techniques. Our flights required long walks into terminals and transportation to the tarmac by bus.

• Expect some international programming on Chinese televisions.

• Expect electrical outages – especially in rural areas. Electrical power is a precious commodity and periodically is terminated without notice to conserve power because of heavy demand and expense.

• Expect automobile drivers to move more erratically than what is customary even on most United States roads. Expect "close calls" with trucks, buses, automobiles, "pull-carts," bicycles and pedestrians, who coexist in the streets.

• Expect hair-raising taxi rides with constant horn blowing and sometimes shouting.

• Expect good service, a positive work ethic, and a high level of energy among service workers in the hotels and restaurants. They are eager to please. Workers knew why I was there and were happy that we were helping girls from their country.

• Expect older buildings – some without modern heating, ventilation, or air-conditioning (HVAC) systems. Older, tired-looking decor in the hotels is typical. (except "The White Swan" in Guangzhou). The temperatures may not be as comfortable in some of the older buildings nor be sophisticated due to a cultural preference and/or the economic profile of the province.

• Expect differences in the department stores. Staff may well be uniformed. There were no automatic cash registers in use in 1996 --

an abacus and cardboard box functioned as the calculator and cash box! Department store decor will appear dated and tired. The department stores will sell small penny hard candy. This was so popular with the 25 children in with our older children's classes and teachers. Chinese writing is on the wrappers!

• Expect a good bit of "down time" (i.e., days) after you get your child while the paperwork is being processed. Use the time to catch up on rest and relaxation as well as to bond with your child. Socialize with newfound friends and enjoy yourself.

• Expect possible sights of extreme poverty (i.e., adults and children begging).

• Expect that children from the same orphanage probably will have the same "surname" and a different nickname to suit their personality or appearance.

• Expect to be able to communicate by pointing! Consider bringing index cards with key translated words to share in China if you are not going to be with an interpreter the entire time.

• Expect to witness positive, healthy lifestyles among the Chinese. The people, on the whole, appear to be fit, trim, and lean. Their diet is high in vegetables, rice, and fruit. Outside exercise classes – especially among "elders"-were commonplace. (There were, however, pockets of heavy smokers among young people that was especially noticeable in public places. There did not appear to be smoking restrictions anywhere.)

Reflection — Compassion

We have all been given resources, and opportunities to serve God and others who are physically or emotionally sick, poor in spirit, or experiencing some difficulty in life. We are expected to do this as if we were trying to help Christ, Himself, with a caring and loving approach. Our response defines who we are, where our hearts are, and how our Lord would be pleased with the way we approach others here on earth in their time of need. (A favorite saying which hangs in my office reads: "What we are is our gift from God, what we become is our gift to Him.")

We influence and choose our causes. One of the most noteworthy "top of mind awareness" we have when deciding to "take on" a need centers around the theme of many sermons and homilies is "if today you hear His voice, harden not your hearts." Related scripture verses that impress me with the concept of compassion and how we are taught to respond to societal problems follow:

    • *For I was hungry and you fed me; I was thirsty and you gave me water...naked and you clothed me; sick and in prison and you visited me...And I, the King, will tell them, "When you did it to these my brothers you were doing it to me!" (Matthew 25:35-36, 40)*

    • *"When He saw the crowds, He had compassion on them, because they were harassed and helpless, like sheep without a shepherd." (Matthew 9:36)*

    • *"But you, O Lord, are a God full of compassion, and gracious, longsuffering and abundant in mercy and truth." (Psalm 86:15)*

"What we are is our gift from God what we become is our gift to Him"

Prayer in Solitude

My Lord God,
I have no idea where I am going.
I do not see the road
ahead of me.
I cannot know for certain
where it will end.
Nor do I really know myself
and the fact that I think
I am following Your will
does not mean that
I am actually doing so.
But I believe
that the desire to please You
does in fact please You.
And I hope
I have that desire
in all that I am doing.
I hope I will never
do anything apart
from that desire.
And I know if I do this,
You will lead me
by the right road
though I may
know nothing about it.
Therefore, I will trust
You always though I may
seem to be lost
and in the shadow of death.
I will not fear,
for You are ever with me,
and will never leave me
to face my perils alone.
                          -Thomas Merton

III.

What We Feel Resulted

Jane Su
July 4, 1995
Changsha, China

joyfully adopted January 30, 1996
Kathy, Jack, Katie and Jonathan Rudnick

"May He grant you your heart's desire and fulfill all your plans."
(Psalm 20:4)

Health Issues

There are special health issues associated with children adopted internationally. These should be considered when the children are being treated by United States physicians and health care professionals who may be unfamiliar with different development and growth "standards" from foreign countries (see Websites "www.fwcc.org" and "www.spafa.org"). Studies have shown that more than 50 percent of internationally adopted children have an undiagnosed medical condition at the time of initial evaluation in the United States. (Judge, 1999) Depending on the country, a variety of concerns about potential problems expressed by parents include:

- Developmental delay
- Fetal alcohol syndrome
- Intestinal parasites
- Tuberculosis
- Hepatitis
- HIV/AIDS
- Stresses of family integration
- Attachment disorder
- Neurological impairment

Reflection

We experienced "parental fear" when we heard that Jane's head circumference did not match the developmental level on a standard U.S. growth chart. While in China, I generally observed that the older girls and women there appeared to be very petite. I now know that there is a different growth chart used for Asian children. Other issues we experienced that may need to be discussed with pediatricians relative to children adopted from foreign countries include crib fear, (once laid down, the children learn that they may not be picked up again for a long while due to so many infants and such little time), dental issues, small narrow feet (fitting shoes), and general petiteness relative to height and low birth weight. Without the benefit of having a medical history to consider the possible sign of sight difficulty, we failed to identify farsightedness and a "lazy eye." We were fortunate that our pediatrician, Theresa Smith, M.D. offers a routine non-invasive "eye screen" with her practice. This detected impaired vision and allowed for immediate intervention with a prescribed temporary patch along with corrective lenses. (The results have been successful.)

Jane is now five years old. We find that it would not have been advisable for her to have been taken "off the bottle" when typically recommended for other infants. It was more important that she receive adequate nutrition than adhere to a recommended weaning schedule. She weighed 10 pounds when I brought her over from China and at present weighs 30 pounds (10th percentile compared with other girls in Southern China.) We are giving Jane a nutritional supplement daily to ensure that she continues her strong physical development. Emotionally, Jane is well adjusted; and, like other Asian children with whom she interacts, is animated, sweet, and has an incredibly adaptive personality. She has a healthy amount of shyness when meeting new people and exhibits humility, confidence, and a strong will. Jane is incredibly appreciative of every little gift or courtesy done for her. It is almost like, (perhaps genetically), that she is aware of her humble beginnings!

There seem to be differences in philosophy among clinicians relative to the time frame for an inter-country adopted child's first visit. One study recommends that a child be evaluated as soon as he or she arrives in the United States. (King and Hamilton, 1997) Another recommends delaying the initial medical visit for two to four weeks unless there is an acute condition, in which case clinical intervention should be sought immediately. (Quarles and Brodie, 1998) The rationale offered is so that the parents and child may have adequate time to adapt to each other.

Based on Jane's situation, my strong recommendation is that an adopted child should be seen immediately after returning home. Jane had thrush, diaper rash, bronchitis, minor sores, and otitis media (ear infections). As a "non-clinical" parent, I was not aware of all of these conditions. Our pediatrician immediately took a blood sample from Jane to rule out the presence of parasites and other possible illness.

To illustrate this rationale, there are two different instances where friends with adopted children learned from physicians that their children had heart conditions, which had previously not been known. One required lifesaving surgery (which was successful); the other is being closely monitored for a heart murmur. Conclusively, I think the benefits of more immediate intervention far outweigh any disadvantage of the practice of obtaining medical services as soon as possible.

"Special Kids"

Because Jane lay in a crib for seven months and had little love, stimulation, or opportunity for muscle development, she was slightly developmentally delayed. Fortunately, we became aware of the "Special Kids and Families" Program through several of Kathy's nursing coworkers and our pediatrician, Dr. David Ziebarth, a loyal supporter of "Special Kids." Not only was this a "Godsend" of a program, but it also really opened our eyes to the challenges facing children and families with long term special needs.

A family-centered program, the "Special Kids" philosophy and mission includes "recognizing the needs of every family member, the value of each person, and that all of us have special abilities." "Special Kids" provides early intervention treatment for children, ages birth to three years, with developmental disabilities. The program and support services involve families in planning and implementing comprehensive treatment services to help children and their families live fuller lives; and, for children to reach their full potential. This is accomplished through a number of available services tailored to meet individual needs including:
• Nutritional counseling
• Wellness education
• Physical medicine and rehabilitation therapies
• Parent/grandparent support counseling
• Advocacy therapy and equipment/toy loan services

We initially felt guilty because there were children (primarily, lovable Down's syndrome children) in the program who were not going to *fully* recover and would require ongoing special support. However, we found that the staff enjoyed this different and new challenge — especially with the differences and uniqueness of treating an Asian child. The staff and families were genuinely concerned with our involvement. We observed that they recognized and witnessed to the potential significance of participants caring for one another – "So in Christ we who are among many from one body and each member belongs to all others." (Romans 12:14,15) The other families with

whom we interacted genuinely welcomed Jane and us for our four month participation. The families enjoyed observing and being part of Jane's rapid progress, development, and success. The program significantly helped Jane with several basic skill sets, such as:
- Holding up her head
- Crawling
- Gross and fine motor skills
- Color and shape recognition and familiarity
- Socialization with others
- Readiness for main-streaming into a local church's preschool play group

Reflection

We learned a great deal about the efforts undertaken and enormous obstacles families of special needs children must overcome to procure necessary services and support. One of the greatest is the gap of services available for many children between the ages of three and five. The participation and heightened awareness contributed to our own personal development and growth, for which we are extremely grateful.

Operation Blanket

Children's Spiritual Growth —

The result of the adoption of Jane on the children was very positive. Katie, with the help of Jonathan, initiated a blanket drive (Operation Blanket). She had a target goal of 100 blankets – 50 for the children in the unheated orphanage in China and 50 for children in a local family homeless shelter. The overwhelming response was 850 blankets collected in an eight-week period. People were eager to donate. Some even handstitched blankets for these causes. Several years later, Jonathan, an avid sports enthusiast, took Jane to practices and games where he proudly "showed her off." She became the honorary team mascot. During games, Jane would "hang out" near the dugout where she was deemed "a good luck charm!" (See sidebars – solicitation letter and "excerpts" from newspaper article.)

The process of adoption helped Katie and Jonathan become more selfless and to grow closer to one another; and to Jane who was a common focus of their love and attention. As well, it helped divert attention from each other and diffuse a normal level of friction and sibling rivalry with the eleven-month age difference between them. It made them more aware of diversity issues and subtle destructive comments of racism and bigotry from their schoolmates. (Jonathan and a female classmate actually had to let a fellow classmate know that the slandering remark made about race, and an off-the-cuff remark about "dirty foreigners" was not appreciated as his new sister whom he greatly loved was a "foreigner.")

Blanket Solicitation Letter

40 Timber View Cove
Cordova, TN 38018

Dear

I am writing to ask your support, if you can, for a project I am undertaking. The cold months will be here before we know it. With the recent adoption of my sister, Jane, from China, I realized that there are both children here and in China that are not fortunate enough to have adequate clothes and blankets for warmth.

"Operation Blanket" is what I am calling my effort. My goal is to collect 100 blankets – preferably new – 50 regular blankets for children here and 50 baby blankets for children in the orphanage in China. My sister lived in an orphanage for six months without heat before she came to our home in America.

If you can, I am asking for you to donate one blanket, (tax deductible), – new or used. (Please indicate the value of the blanket(s) for an accurate receipt.) You can drop the blanket by my home, my Dad's office at Saint Francis Hospital, or call me at 753-4409 and we will arrange to pick it up. If you cannot, I ask that you pray for those less fortunate for us. I would like to get the blankets by October 1 so I can distribute them here and arrange to send them to China. Here, I will get the blankets to Mr. Tom Wilson for the homeless children in the Final Net Program. In China, they will go to the Changsha Social Welfare Orphanage in the Southern Hunan Province through the Mid-South Christian Services Adoption Agency.

Thank you very much for considering this request.

Sincerely,

Kathleen (Katie) C. Rudnick

(Excerpts from *Common Sense* (West Tennessee Catholic Diocese of Memphis, TN, November 1996)

"OPERATION BLANKET EXCEEDS EXPECTATION"—
YOUTH GUEST COLUMN

My newly adopted sister lived in an unheated orphanage. She was very cold like the other 49 babies, sick, and almost dying. When my dad got her, it changed our lives completely. We thought it would be a good project if we sent 50 blankets to Changsha, China and we heard of a program right here in Memphis called the FINAL NET program for homeless women and children. We also sent out a letter that most of you may have received.

We received approximately 600 baby blankets, and about 250 adult blankets. People brought them to my dad's office, our parish, or our home.

As you fall into bed each night from this day forward, you can sleep knowing that babies in China and women and children here in Memphis are sleeping right now nice and warm. May God bless you always!

Thanks for your support,
Kathleen C. Rudnick

Final Net

The Homeless Children's Program

October 22, 1996

St. Benedict at Auburndale School
2100 North Germantown Parkway
Cordova, TN 38018

To Whom It May Concern:

One of your young students has accomplished a remarkable service. Katie Rudnick recently collected 85 blankets (thus far) for homeless Memphians. An equal number of blankets have also been collected and are being shipped courtesy Federal Express to an orphanage in China.

For a twelve year old to conceive the idea and follow through collecting and delivering such a project is mind boggling. The compassion, dedication and perseverance Katie has shown is very rare. A wonderful future for her is easily predicted.

Special commendations should be awarded to Katie's church for her spiritual formation and to her school for her education. In addition, a very special award should go to the Rudnick family for the love and values instilled in Katie.

Katie's inspiration came from her little sister, Jane Su, whose first months were spent in the ill equipped home where the blankets are being shipped. Perseverance and other family support came from her brother Jonathan and from loving parents, Jack and Kathie Rudnick.

We at Final Net receive our support from the community as we work with the homeless. Never before have we received such a magnificent gift from anyone so young.

Sincerely,
Dana M. Peck
Director

Prejudice/Injustice

When Janet Lawrence conducted our home study as part of the process, she routinely advised us that because we were now going to be an interracial family, through our international adoption; and that we might experience some prejudicial behavior toward the new child and our family. Despite the warning, we were quite surprised when we encountered a taste of this just two short months after Jane arrived in the United States. One day, Jane accompanied Kathy on an errand to a tailor shop. The proprietor "made over" Jane and acknowledged her beauty. The proprietor then, matter of factly, asked when Kathy was planning to have Jane's eyes "fixed." The proprietor told Kathy that she had read about this and that it could easily be done. When Kathy politely asked, with restrained disbelief, why she would ask that, the woman replied "…Well you want her to look more American, don't you?" Kathy replied that Jane was quite beautiful the way she is and Kathy had no reason to want to rob Jane of her God-given heritage and look. "If you see oppression of the poor and violation of rights and justice, do not be shocked…" (Ecclesiastes 5:7) Again, Kathy was thinking, spiritually, that God created us all in his image and likeness — a tenet that is central to the positive opportunity to practice and witness to our faith and belief that we are all coheirs to the Kingdom of God.

Reflection

We strongly feel that this was honest ignorance on the part of this woman.

The lesson we learned is to be sensitive to what people say but understand and respond appropriately. There is a time and opportunity to witness to our faith and offer information that may prompt the person to pause, reflect, and reassess their feelings. We are products of our environment. If people are raised in a "controlled" or sheltered environment, there is no communication opportunity to influence their opinion otherwise. When someone does not know better, we may need to give the benefit of the doubt and firmly witness to the moral religious principle we feel should govern a situation.

Reflection

If someone were to take a look at injustices in the United States, they would find significant opportunities for improvement. Such areas include:

• Care for the elderly
• Day care for children
• Abortion and euthanasia sentiments
• Treatment and support for the developmentally disabled—children and adults.

Prejudice and injustices unfortunately, have been woven into the fabric of the United States over many years. Discrimination on the basis of race and ethnicity continues to exist.

Our family's outlook has become more global. This awareness has prompted us to increase charitable donations to formerly unknown needy groups. This newfound diversity and outlook have helped enrich our growth as individuals, as a family, and has prompted us to make an extra effort to contribute to improving our community.

Reflection — Prejudice/Injustice

• *"...render justice to the afflicted and needy, rescue the lowly and the poor..." (Psalms 82:3,4)*

• *"Those who tell lies to one another speak with deceiving lips and a double heart." (Psalms 12:3)*

• *"Learn to do good, make justice your aim...hear the orphan's plea..." (Isaiah 1:17)*

• *"Do not exploit or ill treat the stranger, the orphan, or the widow." (Jeremiah 22:3,4)*

After Jane and I arrived back in the United States, there were humorous inquiries from children when they met her. We surmised that these were consistent with a scriptural message, "...Anyone who will not receive the Kingdom of God like a little child will never enter it." (Mark 10:15) These questions included:

• When she gets older, should we tell her she is adopted?
• Will she be good at karate?
• When she starts to talk, will it come out in Chinese?

- Where is her real mother?
- Why doesn't she look like her mom?
- Does she like rice?
- When she smiles, can she see?

We consider these to be innocent humorous remarks without negative intent. Surprisingly, many adults think along these same lines as well!

Children, unfortunately, learn about stereotyping and prejudice at an early age. One night at dinner, my son, Jonathan, (then 10 years old) seemed a little down. When we asked him what was the matter, he said, "I am worried that Jane will never get married. She looks very different. Will anyone want to go out with her since she is Chinese?"

This was an educational opportunity for us to share with our two children that they have a new role as older siblings – to teach, watch out for, and protect their younger sister. We shared that unfortunately, they might experience some children making fun of Jane because she is different. With the added joy and excitement of another new member of our family come other responsibilities associated with this as well. Our children do realize the special opportunity to witness to ideals about which they have been taught. We predict that, while difficult at times, this experience will help them grow as individuals and sensitize them to future situations where their lives will be meaningful and make a difference in the environments they can influence.

Reflection
Jane is beginning to realize that she is different looking than almost everyone else living in our community. My wife had to laugh recently when she recounted a conversation between Jane and another child on the playground. The child asked Jane where her real mother was…when Jane pointed, proudly, to Kathy, the child said "…Well you don't look like her." Without hesitation, Jane replied, "I know she doesn't look like me – I look like my father – we both have dark hair!"

In another encounter Jane asked Kathy why they looked different from one another. Kathy braced herself for an involved explanation of the adoption and just simply replied "...that is the way God made us." Jane accepted this explanation temporarily and then asked "why do you and daddy have big such butts?" Kathy again repeated "...that is the way God made us." Persistent, Jane said "I think I would like to have a big butt like you both have..." Kathy ended this by sharing that she (Jane) would look pretty foolish if she had big butts like ours!

"Let the little children come to me and do not hinder them, for the Kingdom of God belongs to such as these." (Luke 18:16)

Reflection

It is very natural for children to want to belong, feel connected, and fit in. Humor takes the edge off of the challenging "differences questions" we will encounter in a world where prejudice, racism, bigotry, and injustices continue to exist.

Birthmother's Courage

The central earthly figure of Jane's story, a triad of relationships among the birth parents, Jane, and us is really Jane's biological mother. The vital role played by mothers in the emotional bonding resulting from carrying a child through pregnancy evokes powerful images of care and nurturing.

I have already touched on the historical and cultural circumstances affecting the endangered females in China. As referenced in my journal, the police report reviewed by the American Consulate during Jane's exit visa processing and in Guangzhou, China suggested that the length of time between Jane's birth and her abandonment (12 days) presupposes that the birth mother, most likely, struggled emotionally with the decision to give Jane up.

At a very minimum, Jane's Birthmother fulfilled God's test of love by intuitively complying with the Biblical command "Choose life…" (Deuteronomy 30:19)

We feel that Jane's biological mother truly loved her and experienced deep physical and emotional pain over this difficult decision. We reflect on the passion of the birth mother not only at separation from Jane, but the nine months of emotional uncertainty as to whether the baby was a boy or girl; and anticipating the dreaded abandonment she knew she might face must have been agonizing. I cannot help but sympathize and acknowledge the pain Jane's Birthmother undoubtedly felt when parting from Jane. She set Jane down on the side of a busy road and probably watched from afar to ensure that she was safely found and delivered to the police station where she hopefully would begin the process toward a better life. No matter how we imagine the many possible scenarios, variables, and circumstances surrounding the set of decision options, it all points toward the courage to make a decision to choose life despite probable risky odds. She also exhibited selflessness by wanting Jane to grow up with better resources and circumstances to have a better life.

There is a powerful scripture which links parallel similarities between Jane and her biological mother had with Moses and his mother relative to adoption and birth. "When she (Moses' mother) could hide him (Moses) no longer, she took a papyrus basket...and putting the child in it placed it among the reeds...His sister stationed herself at a distance to find out what would happen to him...she (Pharaoh's daughter)...adopted him as her son." (Exodus 2:3-4, 10)

Another story recounted in the Bible relates to King Solomon, who recognized the powerful instinctive love and bond between a mother and a child; and, that a true mother would never, willingly, allow or relinquish her child to someone else without it being in the child's best interest. (1 Kings 3:26-28) Unconditional love prompts a birth mother to lovingly give up such a precious gift through adoption.

Consider for a moment, some of the powerful emotions we felt when separated for a period of time from a parent or loved one early on in life. Thomas Brosnan in "The Spirituality of Adoption" shares that even though adoption brings many blessings, there still exists some terror every adopted person experiences when separated from his or her mother. (Brosnan, 1992) Ironically in order to achieve this blessing, abandonment or relinquishment is always the basic foundation of the adoption experience.

Parents can certainly relate to the momentary panic when a child wanders off in a department store or a crowded public place. Consider the separation from a flesh and blood relative early in life relative to marked anxiousness.

Baptism

"Those who accepted his message were baptized." (Acts 2:4)

Jane's baptism was a special event. In addition to family, we had 200 friends from church, work, the children's school, and our neighborhood. So many wanted to share in the joy of spiritually welcoming Jane through the ritual of this sacramental experience. Because of the unique circumstances surrounding Jane's arrival in the United States, her baptism was truly a special event.

Baptism signals new life and a new beginning. When parents bring children to church, they are reminded that this child is not their own property — but a gift from God entrusted to them while here on earth, given to a community and part of His much larger family. We are a community of believers and through baptism we maintain a connectedness with each other through God.

Reflection

Through the ongoing sacramental cycles of life, the growth of our individual spirituality and the application of God's teachings, we enrich our lives and bring deeper meaning to our purpose and existence. We feel fortunate to have experienced this "connectedness" made possible through new life, our faith, and religious customs.

Jane's Baptismal Day
March 3, 1996

The following excerpt from Janc's baptism program profiles a synopsis of Jane's special occasion:

EXCERPT FROM JANE'S BAPTISM PROGRAM

Thank you for sharing and participating in the Sacrament of Baptism for Jane. The special circumstances surrounding her arrival help make this an even more joyous occasion.

As many of you already know, Jane was born in the Hunan province, rural south-central China, on July 4, 1995. She was abandoned on July 16, 1995 and taken to a police station before being placed in an orphanage. Typically, "girl babies" are abandoned a day or two after birth if they are not wanted by the parents. Jane's Chinese name - - Su Qing (Ching) — means clean and white—given to her because she was clean and well cared for when found and has a fair complexion. The twelve-day lapse between birth and abandonment is suggestive of the pattern that the natural mother wanted to keep the baby and struggled with the pressure brought by the husband and/or mother-in-law. We are grateful that Jane's mother "chose life" and pray that she finds peace with her decision.

Our sincere thanks to so many who prayed for our family and supported us during this process. The songs, readings and intentions were selected to reflect our devotion and gratitude to Our Lord, the Blessed Mother, and the special patron saints we invoked.
We appreciate your welcoming Jane home to America!

> Gratefully,
> Kathy, Jack, Katie and Jonathan

Adoptive Family

From a Biblical perspective we have a truly perfect example of an adoptive family in the Holy Family – Jesus, Mary, and Joseph. Joseph was the (adoptive) father of Our Lord. My impression of God's message communicated through scripture, is that a child in an adoptive family is afforded the same level of entitlement as if they were with the family where a child is a product of a biological couple. Through the power and presence of the Holy Spirit we are God's children – created equally – *all* adopted heirs to the Kingdom of Heaven. (Romans 8:16)

Joseph willingly accepted and followed God's direction for him . Joseph chose to be obedient to God even when confronted with a most difficult set of circumstances. Joseph wanted to quietly divorce Mary because he felt her pregnancy resulted from infidelity; however, through an annunciation, he prayerfully chose to listen to the angel who shared that Mary was pregnant through the power of the Holy Spirit – Joseph was faithful to his special calling. (Matthew 1:19-24)

Joseph never preached a sermon, he was not a martyr, and he was not credited with uttering a single word in the Bible. He was a gentle, quiet man who taught and provided for the Maker of the Universe. A carpenter by trade, I have heard it said that as an ordinary man, he (symbolically) bound the Holy Family together with carpenters' glue. He used his talents and skills to craft himself in a manner that was pleasing to God. Joseph is a model father figure whose traits one should want to emulate.

Reflection
It is interesting to note that an additional message we can learn from this is that God achieves great things through ordinary people. St. Terese of Liseux is credited with the adage "Do the ordinary things extraordinarily well" in order to please God with our actions. God uses both ordinary persons and simple things to perform miracles.

Outcomes - What has resulted

The following summarizes thoughts and select results from our adoption. These contain the personal fears and initial misperceptions we experienced.

• Emotionally, with regard to time, fears concerning inability to be available enough to our other two children time-wise, were unfounded. In fact, it is just the opposite! It has brought us all closer together with Jane as a common focus.

• Ongoing financial concerns (i.e., beyond the initial outlay expenses) with a third child are unfounded. We have not felt a great sacrifice to absorb Jane's expenses. Five can eat, virtually, as inexpensively as four (excluding eating out)! The generosity and gifts

Jane with Katie and Jonathan, Cape Cod, 1999

given to us have defrayed a good bit of the clothing and toy expenses. Play school/child care have been paid for though "cafeteria plan" pretax dollars.

• Our spiritual lives have been enriched. This is in response to our feelings of gratitude for the precious gift bestowed on us as well as an ability to now spiritually relate, firsthand, to many of the messages offered through scripture. The church communities with which we have been associated have been incredibly helpful and supportive.

• Physically, and emotionally, we do expend additional energy caring for Jane. This is normal. We have found, however, that God gave us the strength, resources, and stamina to handle the additional activity of an infant and toddler.

• At least nine additional adoptions have been completed or are within several months of completion resulting from others seeing Jane or hearing about her story.

• We have an increased global awareness of human-rights needs worldwide. The community support from adoptive families helps retain and foster a cultural heritage for the children and their families (as well as establishing a network of good friends with values similar to and in common with ours.)

• An enrichment has touched our "extended family" through her radiating presence! (see photographs)

• Through my presentations in writing and in person, there is a broadened awareness and intrigue with the plight of international children awaiting placement in loving homes through adoption.

• A spiritual coalescing through the sacrament of Baptism took place with our child coming to the U.S. and our community.

• We have a heightened appreciation for our citizenship and privilege of living in the U.S. Having worked through the immigration system and processes, as citizens, we have much to be grateful for.

• A normal feeling of concern continues relative to a lack of awareness or knowledge of Jane's genetic make-up, history of any illnesses, and predisposition to illnesses and/or compromising health issues.

• We feel privileged to have been called to serve. It has prompted us to become more involved in pro-life organizations and to help promote causes that support life (through all ranges of the age continuum).

• From an investment perspective, financial savings early on in our married life paid dividends with monies being available to embark on the adoption journey. When we began saving for retirement, we had no idea that we might need to invoke the no penalty loan provision against our tax-sheltered annuity for a non-retirement/emergency reason. (i.e. adoption)

• From an influence on business and human resource policy development perspective, an adoption benefits (similar to one established by Tenet Health System who helped with our adoption of Jane) was developed and implemented at West Tennessee Healthcare (WTH) (See appendix). As of this writing, four adoptions at WTH have been completed (within the first 18 months of implementation) by employees. This was made possible from the financial support of the organization through this new policy. Presentations to community civic groups have prompted and challenged the thought processes of the one hundred some business leaders in the area to consider a similar benefit for their organization to encourage adoption among employees.

• We gained an awareness of the complex (legal) juvenile adoption processes which are in place for the purpose of safeguarding and

Jane with proud relatives, the John Rudnicks.

Jane with proud relatives, the Edward Cranleys.

advocating for immigrants entering the U.S. It also highlighted the differences and varying requirements for re-adoption among the states relative to how each state recognizes the finalization of adoption.

• We realize that adopted children who are loved are special.

• We have a heightened awareness of the global apostolic need fulfilled by missionaries, such as Mother Teresa, and all who serve among the poor.

• We experience the unique opportunity to be part of an interracial family and the associated diversity. This allows us to maintain a sensitivity to the complex challenges of racism, prejudice, and religious bigotry which still exist, and allow us to have more of a bond of "connectedness" with our global fellow men.

• We realize the need for a reexamination and reordering of life's priorities. I have found a renewed desire to get home more quickly at the end of the day to spend time with the family. (For those appointments over which I have control, I do not schedule evening meetings unless absolutely necessary.)

Re-Adoption

Re-adoption means "adopting again" in the United States after returning "home" from another country.

There are several reasons why re-adoption after returning from another country is advisable. Despite the fact that Tennessee, for example, recognizes the finalization of adoption when completed in another country (China), other states throughout the union do not.

Re-adoption solidifies the child's status in the United States especially if the family moves to another state within the United States where re-adoption is required. The process is not difficult. It requires a perfunctory court appearance before a judge. An attorney who specializes in re-adoption proceedings is strongly advised. Costs, at the time of our re-adoption approximated $1,000.00 including legal fees.

Citizenship

There is a structured process established by the Immigration Services (INS) to apply for the citizenship of internationally adopted children. At the beginning of the process, we assumed that Jane would be a citizen by virtue of *our* citizenship. However, that is not the case.

For us, the citizenship process took about 22 months. It has recently been streamlined to as little as four months. We had our local congressman, John Tanner and his office, follow through on the application. This

was very beneficial relative to tracking and knowing the whereabouts and status of the application. It is called a "congressional tag." It is strongly recommended that you contact your local congressman. This is typically a service that they will provide. "Blessed is the nation whose God is the Lord!" (Psalm 86:10)

Jane with Katelyn Shaner, Citizeship Day, February 6, 1999.

Coincidence

Shortly after my return home from China, we welcomed a new Chief Financial Officer, Ed Bode, to our home for dinner. We enjoyed getting to know Ed and acquainting him with different parts of the city as he considered where to settle his family, then still in Middle Tennessee. Ed was enamored with the story of Jane, her presence, and the special charm she seemed to exude.

When I shared with Ed the story of arranging the finances for the adoption and the costs (i.e., primarily through the 403(b) no penalty loan), almost as an afterthought Ed asked if I had taken advantage of the company's $2,500 adoption benefit. I shared that I knew nothing about this, but would inquire. The following week I learned that I was eligible and provided appropriate documentation for fund approval. When I received this several weeks later, I immediately applied the after-tax amount to the outstanding loan.

Reflection

Once again, God demonstrated the message for us to trust Him and not to let finances stand in the way of adoption. If you have your heart in the right place and you pray, the path that our Lord wants us to follow will be made clear. Either the doors will open and the appropriate resources provided for, or signs and circumstances would be evident that we were not meant to go down "that" road, and we continue discerning God's plan for the remainder of our journey here on earth.

What I Would and Would Not Change

One of the questions I receive occasionally is "…what mistakes might you have made; and, if you had to do it over again, what would you do differently?" I have read that mistakes are only committed if you learn nothing from the experience. While there is no doubt I made many mistakes, I feel I did learn a great deal! Accordingly, I will focus only on what I would and would not change:

Several of the following items have already been built into improving the process by the adoption agency we used. My responses to what I would change follow:

• A better communication process for "the strangers" whose adoption has been arranged for those traveling from all over the country making a pilgrimage overseas at the same time. The dynamics of group process need to be established relative to expectations, problem resolution, and level of interdependence desired. A structure and review should be in place with group members. As, in any situation, it is difficult to bring a group of strangers together and in a short period of time fulfill a task or mission without a smooth process. (This is especially the case with as emotionally-charged a process as is involved.)

• A more comprehensive orientation understanding of culture, norms, nuances, and expectations would ease anxiety about travel to a foreign country for many.

• I would have made a more conscious effort to have more short term savings during our marriage. I wish I had searched for more information about adoption from China sooner to expedite our data collection process with the notion that an adoption may have occurred earlier. We were fortunate to have access, without penalty, to our long-term savings when the opportunity (need) knocked. If we had more liquid savings, we might have considered doing this earlier, and possibly even again!

• On one hand, I would have lobbied the agency for translation support during the entire time while in China. It was a precarious and scary situation at times. (The flip side, however, was somewhat of a character-building experience with the constant need to rely on faith and prayer during the process. This also fostered an interdependence among the group which helped build relationships for several of us.)

• I would have brought more baby support items to leave for use in the orphanage; and, would have been better prepared for the types of minor illnesses encountered. Perhaps if I had a written algorithm of symptoms for more direct and aggressive treatment, earlier intervention might have eased Jane's pain sooner (if I had known what to look for and what to do).

• I would not worry as much about the financial dimension of the process as the foremost issue. Granted, "no money no mission"- - and while we were fortunate enough to have "means," those who do not need to realize that there are church members, foundations, and generous humanitarians who would help fund an effort should the desire exist.

• I would have made more of an effort to prepare the dog for the transition of a strange child, Jane, into our home. The dog was confused and puzzled with a new person in the house and barked, generally, for two days!

• I would have been more resigned to the will of God through prayer - - especially during the anxious high spots of the process both in the United States and in China.

• I would have brought a relative along as it was somewhat difficult to be alone (although I had enormous help from our friends in the group); but, as with the Apostle Thomas, words, pictures, and videos only capture what it "must have been like." It is not the same as being there!

• I would have ensured that we have a copy of notarized original seal documents of the significant aspects of our lives - - birth, marriage, etc. for the entire family. Since we had all our significant activities out of state, it took a bit more effort to fulfill document requirements.

I would not change:
• The decision to proceed.
• The decision to have Kathy stay home to stabilize the household.
• Seeing a pediatrician immediately.
• Scheduling Jane's baptism as soon as possible.

• Involving all our various communities in the joy and excitement of the process - - before, during, and after.

• Naming Jane after a relative.

• Keeping Jane's given surname as her middle name.

• "Showing Jane off" and bring her out as much as possible!

• Buying as much in China for her to appreciate her heritage later in life.

• The heavy reliance of faith, prayer, and trust in God.

Conclusion

Little did I know that the poem I memorized in the eighth grade while a student at Boston Latin School that excerpts from "The Road Not Taken" by Robert Frost, (Lathem, 1969), would have a very significant meaning later in life:

The Road Not Taken

Two roads diverged into a yellowed wood,
And sorry I could not travel both
And be one traveler, long as I stood
And looked down one as far as I could
To where it bent in the undergrowth;

Then took the other, just as fair
And having perhaps the better claim,
Because it was grassy and wanted wear;
Though as for that the passing there
Had worn them really about the same,

And both that morning equally lay
In leaves no ste had trodden black.
Oh, I kept the first for another day!
Yet knowing how way leads on to way,
I doubted if I should ever come back.

I shall be telling this with a sigh
Somewhere ages and ages hence:
Two roads diverged in a wood, and I –
I took the one less traveled by,
And that has made all the difference.
                                    Robert Frost

Our decision to adopt was a bit unusual and challenged us to pause and wonder about some of the decisions we made and the

120

amount of risk we had taken for enriched and more fulfilling lives. The journey to adoption was our road less traveled. "I will proclaim the decree of the Lord. You are my child. This day I have fathered you." (Psalm 2:7)

We are grateful to God for His indescribable gift.

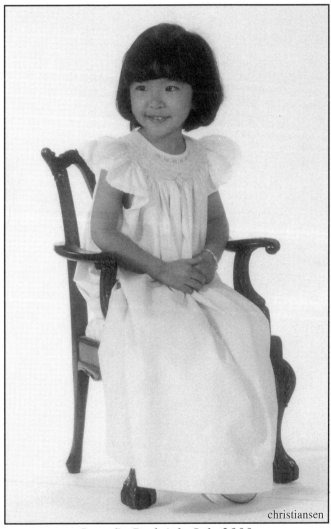

Jane Su Rudnick, July 2000

Appendix

International Adoption Process

Initial inquiry & initial information received

Information meeting between prospective parents and agency representative/ Application received

Completed forms returned to office

Pre-file with INS (Immigration services) - application; fingerprints

A

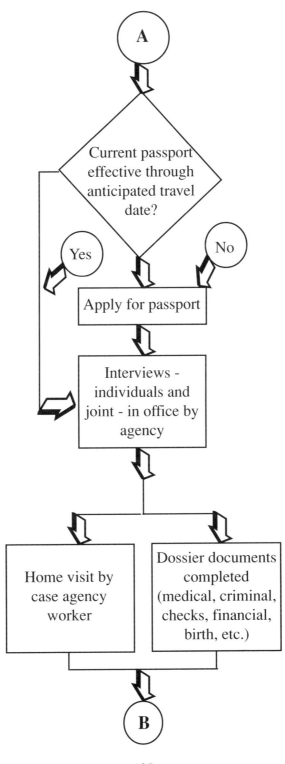

A

Current passport effective through anticipated travel date?

Yes

No

Apply for passport

Interviews - individuals and joint - in office by agency

Home visit by case agency worker

Dossier documents completed (medical, criminal, checks, financial, birth, etc.)

B

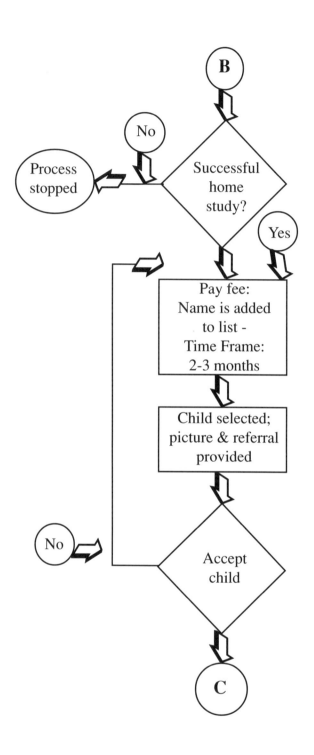

B

Successful home study?

No → Process stopped

Yes

Pay fee:
Name is added
to list -
Time Frame:
2-3 months

Child selected;
picture & referral
provided

Accept child

No

C

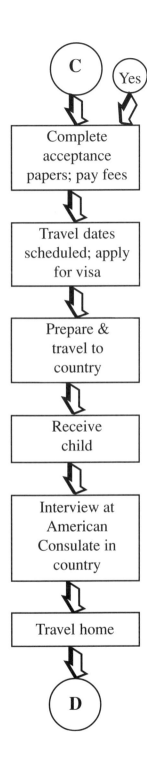

C Yes

Complete acceptance papers; pay fees

Travel dates scheduled; apply for visa

Prepare & travel to country

Receive child

Interview at American Consulate in country

Travel home

D

D

Apply for
re-adoption

Re-adoption
approved

Apply for
citizenship

Post-placement
interviews &
visits according
to country (6
mos.; 1 year, etc.)

Provide picture
of child to
agency during
interviews for
post-placement
reports to foreign
country

Happily
ever
after!!

-Beverly Ward, Debby Stockwell, 2000.

128

WEST TENNESSEE HEALTHCARE MANAGEMENT GUIDEBOOK POLICY

SUBJECT: Adoption Reimbursement Benefit	**POLICY No.: 6000**
APPLICATION: System Wide	**PAGE(s): 1 of 2**
DEPT. RESPONSIBLE: Human Resources	**EFFECTIVE: 07/01/98**
	REVIEWED:
	REVISED:
APPROVED BY:	
	President/CEO	**Date:**

POLICY:

West Tennessee Healthcare has developed a policy to provide eligible employees with some financial assistance incurred during the adoption process.

ELIGIBILITY:

Full time employees of West Tennessee Healthcare are eligible for adoption beneefits after one (1) years of continuous full time employment. The child to be adopted may not be a biological child of either parent. Eligibility is limited to one parent, if both parents are employees of West Tennessee Healthcare.

FINANCIAL REIMBURSEMENT:

Eligible adoption related expenses are reimbursed up to a maximum of $2,000 per child. The child to be adopted must be under 18 years of age for the parent to qualify for financial reimbursement. Financial reimbursement will be subject to the Coordination of Benefits as stated later in this policy. Most expenses directly related to a successul adoption are reimbursable, provided necessary receipts are provided. Items that are reimbursable are:

- Agency and placement fees
- Legal fees and court costs

- Medical expenses of the birth mother
- Medical expenses of the child prior to adoption
- Temporary foster care cost
- Immigration, immunization and translation fees
- Transportation and lodging expenses

<u>Adoption benefit reimbursements are considered taxable income:</u>

The eligible employee may utilize PET time pre-adoption. PET Sick Leave or Prior Sick Leave of up to 4 weeks may be utilized post-adoption, if available. West Tennessee Healthcare recognizes tyhat the adoption process may require time off from work for mandated home studies or travel to a foreign country. Employees are requested to provide their director with as much preliminary information on need for time off as early as possible. This will prevent unplanned interruptions in the work of the department while allowing the employee to take necessary leave time.

COORDINATION OF BENEFITS: You may add your child to your medical, dental, and/or vision insurance at the time of placement. Additions to your benefit plan must occur within 30 days of placement in your home. You will need completed change forms and a copy of the adoption agreement to enroll your child.

In instances where different companies that provide Financial Reimbursement for adoptions employ parents, the benefit must be coordinated betwen the two companies. The parent whose birthday falls first in the calendar year will be considered primary and the other parent will be secondary. The company of the primary parent will pay first and then the company of the secondary parent will pay. In no event will our employees be eligible for more than $2,000 from the combined payments of the two companies.

WEST TENNESSEE HEALTHCARE
Adoption Assistance Reimbursement Request Form

Employee Information:

Employee Name:_____ Emp. #_____ Social Security #_____

Address_____ City, St., Zip_____

Home Telephone #_____ Work Telephone #_____

Eligible Adoption Expense:

Date Paid	Amount	Description of Expense
_____	_____	_____
_____	_____	_____
_____	_____	_____
_____	_____	_____
_____	_____	_____

Total Reimbursement _____

Note:
- Please attach receipts in U.S. dollars for all expenses listed above.
- Please attach a copy of the adoption placement decree.
- Applicable federal taxes will be withheld from your reimbursemnt.

Employee Request for Reimbursement:

I would like to apply for reimbursement of adoption expenses listed above, confirming that:

Child's Name_____ , whose birth date is_____ ,
was placed in my home for the purpose of adoption on_____.
The date for adoption finalization is_____.

I certify that this is a claim for allowable expenses under the West Tennessee Healthcare Adoption Reimbursement Program.

Signature_____ Date _____

Select References

BOOKS

Broderick, Robert C., ed. *The Catholic Study Bible*. New York: Oxford University Press, 1986.

Crim, Keith, ed. *The Perennial Dictionary of World Religions*. San Francisco: Harper and Row, 1989.

Halberstam, Yitta and Leventhal, Judith. *Small Miracles. Extraordinary Coincidences From Everyday Life*. Holbrook, Massachusetts: Adams Media Corporation, 1997.

Kushner, Harold. *How Good Do I Have to Be?* New York: Simon and Schuster, 1997

Kushner, Harold. *When All You've Ever Wanted Isn't Enough*. New York: Simon and Schustler, 1987.

Kushner, Harold. *When Bad Things Happen to Good People*. New York: Simon and Schuster, 1994.

Lathem, Edward Connery, ed. *The Poetry of Robert Frost*. New York: Henry Holt and Co., 1969.

Martin, Ralph. *Called to Holiness. What It Means to Encounter The Living God*. San Francisco: Ignatius Press, 1999.

Merton, Thomas. *The Seven Story Mountain*. Orlando: Harbrace Publishing Company, 1998.

The New American Bible. Catholic Book Publishing Co.: New York, 1970.

Nouwen, Henri J.M. *Adam; God's Beloved* Mary Knoll, N.Y.: Orbis Books, 1997.

Nouwen, Henri J.M. *The Road to Daybreak. A Spiritual Journey.* New York: Doubleday, 1988.

Nouwen, Henri J.M. *The Wounded Healer.* New York: Doubleday, 1979.

Peck, Robert Newton. *Secrets of the Successful Fiction.* Seattle: Roman Books, 1980.

Peck, M. Scott. *The Road Less Traveled*, 2nd ed. New York: Simon and Schuster, 1998.

Peck, M. Scott. *The Road Less Traveled and Beyond. Spiritual Growth in an Age of Anxiety.* New York: Simon and Schuster, 1997.

Powell, S.J., John. *Touched by God. My Pilgrimage of Prayer.* Allen, Texas: Thomas More Publishing, 1999.

Ramsey, Dave. *Financial Peace.* New York: Viking, 1997.

Ramsey, Dave. *More Than Enough.* New York: Viking, 1999.

The Saturday Evening Post Norman Rockwell Book. Indianapolis: The Curtis Publishing Company, Inc., 1997.

Thompson, Frank Charles ed. *The Thompson Chain - Reference Bible New International Version,* Grand Rapids: Zondervan Bible Publishers, 1982.

Zondervan NIV Naves. *The Businessman's Topical Bible.* Kohlenberger, III John R., General Editor. Grand Rapids, Michigan: Zondervan Publishing House, 1992.

ARTICLES

Freundlich, Madolyn. "Families Without Borders." *U.N. Chronicle,* Summer, 1999. 36:2, 88.

Judge, Sharon L. "Eastern European Adoptions: Current Status and Implications for Intervention." *Topics in Early Childhood Education.* 19:4, 1999, pp. 244-252.

King, Patricia and Hamilton, Kendall. "Bringing Kids all the way Home." *Newsweek*, June 16, 1997. 129:24, 60.

Quarles, Christopher S. and Brodie, Jeffrey H. "Primary Care of International Adoptees." *American Family Physicians*, 58:9, December 1998.

Robbins Michael. "The Right Way to Adopt A Baby From Abroad." *Money,* 1997, 26:11, 162.

"The Bible and Adoption." Grand Rapids: Bethany Christian Services, 1998.

ELECTRONIC SOURCES

Brick, Pam. "Made in China." American Medical Association, 1997.

Brosnan, Rev. Thomas. "The Spirituality of Adoption." Baltimore: Adoption Triad Forum, 1992.

Vonk, M. Elizabeth, et al. "Political and Personal Aspects of inter country Adoption of Chinese Children in the United States." Monticore Publishers: 1999.

INTERNET RESOURCES

Bethany Christian Services. (www.bethany.org).

Families With Children from China. (www.fwcc.org).

Southern Piedmont. Adoptive Families of America, Inc. (www.spafa.org).

Special Kids and Families, Inc. (spkids@wnm.net).

Select Index

BK.

The bible &
adoption
grand rapids.

The spir of adop.
Brosnan Rev. Thos

---

article
families w/out
borders
Madolyn.